Deleveraging? What Deleveraging?

Geneva Reports on the World Economy 16

GW00371065

International Center for Monetary and Banking Studies (ICMB)

International Center for Monetary and Banking Studies
2, Chemin Eugène-Rigot
1202 Geneva
Switzerland

Tel: (41 22) 734 9548
Fax: (41 22) 733 3853
Web: www.icmb.ch

Centre for Economic Policy Research

Centre for Economic Policy Research
3rd Floor
77 Bastwick Street
London EC1V 3PZ
UK

Tel: +44 (20) 7183 8801
Fax: +44 (20) 7183 8820
Email: cepr@cepr.org
Web: www.cepr.org

ISBN: 978-1-907142-79-6

Deleveraging? What Deleveraging?

Geneva Reports on the World Economy 16

Luigi Buttiglione
Brevan Howard Investment Products

Philip R. Lane
Trinity College Dublin

Lucrezia Reichlin
London Business School

Vincent Reinhart
Morgan Stanley

ICMB **INTERNATIONAL CENTER FOR MONETARY AND BANKING STUDIES**
CIMB **CENTRE INTERNATIONAL D'ETUDES MONETAIRES ET BANCAIRES**

CEPR PRESS

International Center for Monetary and Banking Studies (ICMB)

The International Centre for Monetary and Banking Studies was created in 1973 as an independent, non-profit foundation. It is associated with Geneva's Graduate Institute of International Studies. Its aim is to foster exchanges of views between the financial sector, central banks and academics on issues of common interest. It is financed through grants from banks, financial institutions and central banks.

The Center sponsors international conferences, public lectures, original research and publications. It has earned a solid reputation in the Swiss and international banking community where it is known for its contribution to bridging the gap between theory and practice in the field of international banking and finance.

In association with CEPR, the Center launched a new series of *Geneva Reports on the World Economy* in 1999. The eleven subsequent volumes have attracted considerable interest among practitioners, policy-makers and scholars working on the reform of international financial architecture.

ICMB is non-partisan and does not take any view on policy. Its publications, including the present report, reflect the opinions of the authors, not of ICMB or any of its sponsoring institutions.

President of the Foundation Board	Thomas Jordan
Director	Charles Wyplosz

Centre for Economic Policy Research (CEPR)

The Centre for Economic Policy Research (CEPR) is a network of almost 900 research economists based mostly in European universities. The Centre's goal is twofold: to promote world-class research, and to get the policy-relevant results into the hands of key decision-makers. CEPR's guiding principle is 'Research excellence with policy relevance'. A registered charity since it was founded in 1983, CEPR is independent of all public and private interest groups. It takes no institutional stand on economic policy matters and its core funding comes from its Institutional Members and sales of publications. Because it draws on such a large network of researchers, its output reflects a broad spectrum of individual viewpoints as well as perspectives drawn from civil society.

CEPR research may include views on policy, but the Executive Committee of the Centre does not give prior review to its publications. The opinions expressed in this report are those of the authors and not those of CEPR.

Chair of the Board	Guillermo de la Dehesa
President	Richard Portes
Director	Richard Baldwin
Research Director	Kevin Hjortshøj O'Rourke

About the Authors

Luigi Buttiglione joined Brevan Howard as Head of Global Strategy in March 2008. Previously, he was Head of Research at Fortress Investment Group (2007-2008). Before joining Fortress, Luigi was Chief Economist at Rubicon Fund Management LLP (2004-2007), Chief Strategist at BlueCrest Asset Management LLP (2003), Head of European Economics at Barclays Capital Securities Limited (2001-2003), a Senior Economist at Deutsche Bank AG (2000-2001) and a Senior Economist at Banca d'Italia (1989-2000). While at Banca d'Italia, he was also a member of the ECB Working Group of Forecasting.

Philip R. Lane is Whately Professor of Political Economy at Trinity College Dublin. He has published widely on financial globalisation, macroeconomic policy and European monetary integration. He has also acted as an academic consultant to a range of international organisations and national central banks. He is a Managing Editor of *Economic Policy* and a Research Fellow of CEPR.

Lucrezia Reichlin is Professor of Economics at London Business School, co-founder and director at now-casting economics limited, board member at Unicredit Banking group and Ageas Insurance. She is an elected fellow of the British Academy and a research fellow of the CEPR. She is the chair of the Scientific Council at Bruegel, the Brussels based think-tank. She has been director general of research at the European Central Bank from 2005 to 2008. Reichlin has published extensively in econometrics where she has pioneered work on the estimation of large dimensional models and in monetary policy.

Vincent Reinhart joined Morgan Stanley in October 2011 as a Managing Director and Chief US Economist. In that capacity, Mr. Reinhart is responsible for the firm's analysis of the US economy. For the four years prior to joining Morgan Stanley, Mr. Reinhart was a resident scholar at the American Enterprise Institute, a nonpartisan think tank located in Washington, DC. He previously spent more than two decades working in the Federal Reserve System, where he held a number of senior positions in the Divisions of Monetary Affairs and International Finance. For the last six years of his Fed career, he served as Director of the Division of Monetary Affairs and secretary and economist of the Federal Open Market Committee. In that capacity, he was the senior staff member providing advice to Fed officials on the appropriate choice and communication of monetary policy. In his research at the Fed and AEI, Mr. Reinhart worked on topics as varied as the conduct and communication of monetary policy, auctions of US Treasury securities, the long-lived consequences of financial crises, and the patterns of international capital flows. At AEI, he frequently commented in the media on the economic outlook and macroeconomic and financial policies.

Acknowledgements

We thank Susan Lund of McKinsey Global Institute for the generous sharing of the data underlying Figures 1.2 and 1.3. We thank Alberto Caruso, Caroline Mehigan, Rogelio Mercado, Sandrine Perret, Alex Redmond, Giovanni Ricco and George Sorg-Langhans for excellent research assistance. Philip Lane also thanks the Institute for New Economic Thinking for a research grant.

Contents

List of Conference Participants

Edmond Alphandéry
Chairman
Centre for European Policy Studies
Brussels

Mourtaza Asad-Syed
Head of Investment Strategy
Société Générale
Geneva

Katrin Assenmacher
Head of Monetary Policy Analysis
Swiss National Bank
Zürich

Vít Bárta
Advisor to Governor
Czech National Bank
Prague

Agnès Bénassy-Quéré
Professor, Ecole d'Economie de Paris, Université
Paris 1
Deputy Chairman, Conseil d'Analyse Economique
Paris

Jan Marc Berk
Division Director
Economic and Research Division
De Nederlandsche Bank NV
Amsterdam

Rémy Bersier
Member of the Executive Board
Banque Julius Baer & Cie SA
Geneva

Laurence Boone
Managing Director
Chief Europe Economist
Bank of America Merrill Lynch
Paris

Claudio Borio
Head of the Monetary and Economic Department
Bank for International Settlements (BIS)
Basel

Luigi Buttiglione
Head of Global Strategy
Brevan Howard Investment Products
Geneva

Mark Carey   Associate Director
                           International Finance
                           Federal Reserve Board
                           Washington, DC

Olli Castrén   Economist
                           Brevan Howard Investment Products
                           Geneva

Benoît Coeuré   Member of the Executive Board
                           European Central Bank
                           Frankfurt am Main

Jean-Pierre Danthine   Vice-Chairman of the Governing Board
                           Swiss National Bank
                           Geneva

Jacques Delpla   Adjunct Professor
                           Toulouse School of Economics

Mathias Dewatripont   Executive Director
                           National Bank of Belgium
                           Brussels

Andreas Dombret   Member of the Executive Board
                           Deutsche Bundesbank
                           Frankfurt am Main

Christophe Donay   Head of Asset Allocation and Macro Research
                           Pictet & Cie
                           Geneva

Steve Donze   Macroeconomist
                           Pictet Asset Management SA
                           Geneva

Federico Fubini   Columnist
                           La Repubblica
                           Rome

Paolo Garonna   Secretary General
                           FEBAF
                           Rome

Patrice Gautry   Chief Economist
                           UBP
                           Geneva

Hans Genberg	Adviser Bank Negara Malaysia
Stefan Gerlach	Deputy Governor Central Bank of Ireland Dublin
Olivier Ginguené	Group Managing Director Pictet Asset Management SA Geneva
Michel Girardin	Lecturer University of Lausanne University of Geneva Founder MacroGuide
Pierre-Olivier Gourinchas	Professor of Economics UC Berkeley
Augusto Hasman	BCC Programme Manager and Economist The Graduate Institute Geneva
Harald Hau	Professor of Economics and Finance Geneva University
Yi Huang	Assistant Professor of Economics & Pictet Chair in Finance and Development The Graduate Institute Geneva
Paul Inderbinen	Deputy Head, Multilateral Affairs State Secretariat for International Financial Matters Basel
Thomas Jordan	Chairman of the Governing Board Swiss National Bank Zürich
Gero Jung	Chief Economist Mirabaud Geneva
Jean Keller	CEO Argos Investment Managers S.A. Geneva

Pierre Keller

Former Senior Partner
Lombard Odier
Geneva

Signe Krogstrup

Deputy Head of Monetary Policy Analysis
Swiss National Bank
Zürich

Jean-Pierre Landau

Professor
Sciences Po
Paris

Valérie Lemaigre

Chief Economist
BCGE
Geneva

Henri Loubergé

Professor of Economics
Geneva University

José Luis Malo de Molina

Director General
Banco de España
Madrid

Alessandro Merli

Frankfurt Correspondent
Il Sole24 Ore
Frankfurt am Main

Ouarda Merrouche

BCC Programme Manager
The Graduate Institute
Geneva

Atif Mian

Professor of Economics and Public Policy
Princeton University

Maurice Monbaron

Member of the Board
Crédit Agricole (Suisse) SA
Geneva

Carlo Monticelli

Head of International Financial Relations
Ministry of Economy and Finance
Rome

Rahul Mukherjee

Assistant Professor
The Graduate Institute
Geneva

Kiyohiko Nishimura

Dean
Graduate School of Economics
University of Tokyo

Fabio Panetta

Deputy Governor-Member of the Governing Board
Banca d'Italia
Roma

Ugo Panizza

Professor of Economics
The Graduate Institute
Geneva

Pierre Pâris

CEO
Banque Pâris Bertrand Sturdza
Geneva

Sandrine Perret

Economist
Brevan Howard Investment Products
Geneva

Adrien Pichoud

Economist
SYZ Asset Management
Geneva

Richard Portes

Professor of Economics
London Business School
President, CEPR

Fabrizio Quirighetti

Chief Economist
SYZ Asset Management
Geneva

Lucrezia Reichlin

Professor of Economics
London Business School

Vincent Reinhart

Economist
Morgan Stanley
New York

Alain Robert

Vice Chairman
Wealth Management
UBS AG
Zürich

Märten Ross

Deputy Secretary General
Ministry of Finance of Estonia

Jean-Pierre Roth

Chairman
Banque Cantonale de Genève
Geneva

Amlan Roy   Managing Director
                                Global Demographics & Pensions Research
                                Crédit Suisse Investment Bank
                                London

Hans-Joerg Rudloff   Chairman
                                Marcuard Holding
                                Zurich

Alexander Swoboda   Professor of Economics Emeritus
                                The Graduate Institute
                                Geneva

Gianluca Tarolli   Market Economist
                                BORDIER & Cie
                                Geneva

Cédric Tille   Professor of International Economics
                                The Graduate Institute
                                Geneva

Angel Ubide   Director of Global Economics
                                D.E. Shaw Group
                                Senior Fellow
                                Peterson Institute for International Economics

Pawel Wyczanski   Advisor, Financial System
                                National Bank of Poland
                                Warsaw

Charles Wyplosz   Professor of International Economics
                                The Graduate Institute
                                Geneva
                                Director ICMB, Geneva

Attilio Zanetti   Head of Economic Analysis
                                Swiss National Bank
                                Zürich

Fritz Zurbruegg   Member of the Governing Board
                                Swiss National Bank

Patrick Zweifel   Chief Economist
                                Pictet Asset Management S.A

Foreword

Since 1999 the Geneva Reports on the World Economy, published jointly by CEPR and ICMB, have informed the highest calibre discussion and debate on global economics issues. The 16th issue delivers on this reputation: the Report provides an in-depth analysis of the role of debt dynamics in the recovery from the global crisis.

The authors' approach is comprehensive and takes into account the changing nature of debt and the way it relates to the global investment position. The report offers not only the context of debt dynamics over the last decade, but also a detailed analysis of the changing nature of debt over time and across the world, the occurrence of leverage cycles, and the capacity for debt and leverage – and the policies to deploy in managing both debt and the legacies of the past crises.

We are very grateful to Luigi Buttiglione, Philip Lane, Lucrezia Reichlin and Vincent Reinhart for work in devising this report, and to the participants of the discussion of the issues raised by this Report that took place on 9 May 2014 for the insights they provide. We are also thankful to the CEPR Publications team and to Anil Shamdasani for their work in making the publication of this report a smooth and professional process.

This report is clear in its outlook: the policy path to less volatile debt dynamics is a narrow one, and it is already clear that developed economies at least must expect prolonged low growth or another crisis along the way. We hope and expect this Geneva Report to make a considerable contribution to the discussion around de-leveraging policy.

Charles Wyplosz, Director, ICMB
Tessa Ogden, Deputy Director, CEPR
August 2014

1 Introduction

1.1 Motivation and main conclusions

After the bankruptcy of Lehman Brothers, the world entered the worst financial crisis since the Great Depression of the 1930s. The crisis affected mainly developed economies: in some cases, in particular the US and the Eurozone, output had already started to contract one year earlier (see the dating by, respectively, the NBER and CEPR). However, after Lehman, the crisis deepened and spread worldwide. The output contraction in the US ended in the third quarter of 2009 but the recovery has been weak. In the Eurozone the situation has been worse, with a double dip in 2011 that seems to have ended only recently. Emerging markets did better during the crisis, but have recently slowed down.

Both the length and depth of the crisis, as well as the weak recovery, cannot be understood without an analysis of the role of debt dynamics. This is the aim of this report. We provide a multi-dimensional perspective on leverage for both advanced and emerging economies. Our comprehensive approach includes both public and private debt, with the latter broken down along sectoral lines (households, non-financial corporates, financial sector). Moreover, we take into account national adding-up constraints by relating sectoral debt levels to the overall international investment position. We examine debt dynamics during the pre-crisis period in developed economies and the subsequent phase of adjustment attempts in recent years. In addition, we highlight a new wave of debt accumulation in emerging markets that has occurred since 2009. In this analysis, we emphasise the macroeconomic impact of leverage, with a sharp distinction between 'normal' recessions, however deep, and the long-lasting impact on the level of output and output growth that can be generated by excessive leverage and financial crises.

Accordingly, the report provides a deep dive into the details of global debt dynamics over the past decade, with consistent comparisons across regions and sectors and an emphasis on the interaction of debt and income. In 2009, half of the economies of the world were in recession and about three quarters of global GDP was in economies that were contracting. The progress of repair since then has been decidedly uneven, importantly related to policy choices. Also, some nations that avoided the direct effects of the financial meltdown have recently built up excesses that raise the odds of a home-grown crisis.

Contrary to widely held beliefs, the world has not yet begun to delever and the global debt-to-GDP is still growing, breaking new highs (see, for example, Figure

1.1). At the same time, in a poisonous combination, world growth and inflation are also lower than previously expected, also – though not only – as a legacy of the past crisis. Deleveraging and slower nominal growth are in many cases interacting in a vicious loop, with the latter making the deleveraging process harder and the former exacerbating the economic slowdown. Moreover, the global capacity to take on debt has been reduced through the combination of slower expansion in real output and lower inflation.

Figure 1.1   World debt

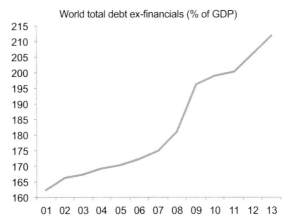

Source: Authors' calculation based on OECD, IMF and national accounts data. See Data Appendix at the end of the report.

Debt capacity in the years to come will depend on future dynamics of output growth, inflation and real interest rates. We argue that potential output growth in developed economies has been on a declining path since the 1980s and that the crisis has caused a further, permanent decline in both the level and growth rate of output. Moreover, we observe that output growth has been slowing since 2008 also in emerging markets, most prominently China. In this context, the equilibrium real interest rate – that is, the interest rate compatible with full employment – is also poised to stay at historical low levels and debt capacity will be under pressure if the actual real rate settles above its equilibrium level. This is likely to be the case in jurisdictions subject to the combined pressure of declining inflation and the zero lower bound constraint. Additional concerns come from possible increases in risk premia in those countries with a high level of legacy debt.

Further insight is provided by Figures 1.2 and 1.3, which show the composition of financial assets for developed markets and emerging markets.[1] The data show that debt-type instruments dwarf equity-type instruments (stock market capitalisation). Moreover, the figures illustrate that the sectoral composition of debt and the relative roles of bank loans versus bonds vary across time and groups.

---

1   These charts focus on the value of financial assets in current dollars at current exchange rates.

In addition, Figures 1.2 and 1.3 vividly show that global debt accumulation was led until 2008 by developed economies. Since then, it has continued under the impulse provided by a sharp rise in the debt levels of emerging economies. This group of countries are a main source of concern in terms of future debt trajectories, especially China and the so-called 'fragile eight', which could host the next leg of the global leverage crisis.

Figure 1.2   The composition of financial assets, developed markets, US$ billion

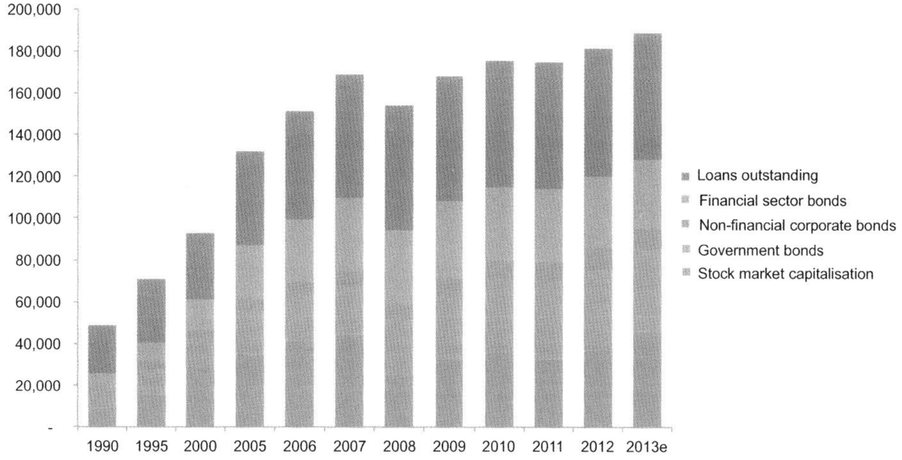

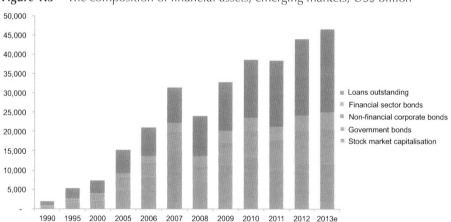

Source: McKinsey Global Institute.

Figure 1.3   The composition of financial assets, emerging markets, US$ billion

Source: McKinsey Global Institute.

Still, the legacy of the past crisis remains severe in developed markets, especially in the peripheral countries of the Eurozone, which remain vulnerable due to the complexity of their crisis and the partial inadequacies of the mix and sequence of the policies adopted. Anglo-Saxon economies – namely, the US and the UK – seem to have managed the trade-off between deleveraging policies and output costs better so far, by avoiding a credit crunch while achieving a meaningful reduction of debt exposure of the private sector and the financial system. This result, however, was achieved at the cost of a substantial re-leveraging of the public sector, including the central banks, whose deleveraging is a primary policy challenge for the years to come.

1.2   Leverage: What we mean by it and why it matters

The concept of leverage has many applications in economics.[2] At the sectoral level, the levels of household debt and corporate debt are much studied in terms of their implications for consumption and investment behaviour. The leverage of financial-sector entities (banks and other types of financial intermediaries) also gives rise to a range of concerns in relation to the incentives facing financial firms and vulnerability to funding shocks. At the sovereign level, the stock of public debt has implications for projected levels of spending and taxation, in addition to determining exposure to financial shocks. Finally, the aggregate level of external debt matters for national macroeconomic performance, with the stock of external debt also an important factor in determining exposure to international funding crises and sudden stops in capital flows.

Of course, the stock of debt has to be assessed in the context of the overall balance sheet. On the liability side, debt gives rise to more concerns if there is only a thin layer of equity liabilities to provide a buffer against losses. On the asset side, debt that is backed by liquid assets with stable returns is less likely to generate repayment problems than debt that is used to fund illiquid assets with volatile returns.

At the same time, a snapshot of a balance sheet is insufficient to conduct a debt sustainability exercise. In particular, the stock of financial assets does not provide a good guide to repayment capacity, since much debt is serviced through future income streams that are not typically capitalised in the balance sheet. For example, household debt may be primarily serviced through wage earnings, while the main asset for most households is non-financial (the family home). Similarly, early-stage firms may have few assets but healthy streams of projected future earnings. For banks, the quality of loan assets is determined by the underlying income streams of their customers. As for the government, it typically has limited financial assets, holds very illiquid non-financial assets and funds debt servicing from future revenue streams.

While taking note of the wide range of other relevant factors, the debt-to-income ratio remains a key metric in assessing debt sustainability. In truth, this

---

2   See also the review of different types of debt overhang provided by Brown and Lane (2011).

is really a proxy for the ratio of debt servicing expenditure to income, which is the ultimate determinant of debt 'affordability' and depends on the average interest rate applied to the debt. In turn, the average interest rate depends on the co-evolution of 'benchmark' risk-free rates and the risk premia that pertain to a given debt category.

Of course, the debt-to-income ratio is not a sufficient statistic, since debts can also be paid off by selling assets. In related fashion, a debtor's willingness to service her debts also depends on her net worth (value of assets minus value of liabilities), especially if her debts are collateralised by her assets such that the debt can be wiped out by transferring assets to her creditors. Accordingly, the fluctuations in net worth that are triggered by shocks to asset prices are an important factor in determining debt sustainability.

In particular, this can give rise to a procyclical dynamic by which rising asset prices improve the net worth of borrowers, permitting the accumulation of extra debt (fuelling further asset price appreciation), whereas a reversal in asset prices is associated with a tightening of debt limits (placing downward pressure on asset prices). This feedback loop between leverage and asset prices is a primary channel linking financial and housing markets with macroeconomic performance.[3] This report will illustrate also how the interaction of asset prices and leverage affected adjustment dynamics during the crisis, especially in the US and the Eurozone.

As noted above, the liability mix between equity and debt is also a key factor in determining debt sustainability. By providing loss absorption capacity, a high equity-to-debt funding ratio reduces the default risk on the debt component. In the household context, the equity-to-debt ratio can be boosted by insisting on significant down payments on housing purchases; for non-financial corporates, the equity-debt mix will be heavily influenced by the structure of the tax system and corporate governance policies; and regulatory policies are a key factor in determining capital-to-asset ratios in the banking sector. In Section 4, we will argue that the delayed recapitalisation of the banking sector in the Eurozone has been one of the causal factors in the very weak credit conditions that have prevailed since 2011.

An excessive level of debt poses both acute and chronic risks. In relation to acute risks, the emergence of concerns about a debtor's willingness or ability to service her debts may lead to a funding crisis, in which creditors are unwilling to extend new loans or rollover existing commitments. Since such concerns may be driven by expectations about a debtor's future ability or willingness to service the debt, there is scope for multiple equilibria in which the beliefs of creditors take on a self-fulfilling quality: if creditors retain confidence, risk premia are low and the debt is sustainable; if panic sets in, risk premia shoot up and the debt is no longer sustainable. In related fashion, a surge in risk premia will also be associated with a sell-off in asset markets, as investors fear that debtors may be forced into fire-sale disposals of assets if debts cannot be rolled over. This confidence-sustainability feedback loop is a key property in evaluating debt levels above some threshold

---

3   See, amongst many others, Adrian et al. (2013), Fostel and Geanakoplos (2013), and Brunnermeier and Sannikov (2014).

level (below which debt levels are safe enough that this feedback loop is not operative).

There is considerable evidence that a high stock of debt increases vulnerability to the risk of a financial crisis.[4] The three main types of crisis are banking crises, sovereign debt crises and external crises (where an economy is unable to rollover its external debt and/or obtain external funding to cover a current account deficit). These crises can occur in isolation or in various combinations (Reinhart and Rogoff, 2009). Moreover, a crisis along one dimension can trigger crises along the other dimensions. For instance, a sudden stop in external funding may induce a wave of bankruptcies that threaten the banking sector, while the (direct and indirect) costs of a banking crisis may generate a sovereign debt crisis. In the other direction, of course, a sovereign debt crisis can undermine the health of the banking system and also lead to non-repayment of foreign liabilities.

Excessive debt levels also can give rise to moral hazard problems and distributional conflicts across sectors. For instance, a government may choose to take over private liabilities, either for efficiency reasons or in response to political pressure. In turn, the anticipation of such fiscal bailouts may lead to lower repayment discipline among private-sector creditors, especially if debt problems are sufficiently widespread in the population to render punishment threats non-credible (Arellano and Kocherlakota, 2014). A similar logic applies if banks are taken into public ownership and private-sector debtors believe that government-owned banks will take a softer line in enforcing repayment. Finally, from a national perspective, the aggregate net international investment position fixes an aggregate resource constraint for the economy: if the aggregate economy is highly indebted vis-à-vis the rest of the world, there is a limit to the effectiveness of domestic policies in shifting debt obligations across sectors. In contrast, a sectoral debt problem in a creditor economy poses fewer risks, since those sectors that have positive levels of net financial assets provide a counterweight to those sectors with stocks of net financial liabilities. This basic consideration illustrates the different implications of high stocks of sovereign debt in creditor countries (such as Japan) versus debtor countries (such as the euro periphery).

Moreover, the 2007-onwards global financial crisis has provided fresh evidence that the resolution of severe crises is extremely costly.[5] At a global level, the advanced economies suffered a severe recession during 2008-10, while the second wave of the crisis in Europe from 2011 onwards further prolonged subpar macroeconomic performance across large parts of the Eurozone. Looking across countries, the severity of the crisis in terms of the decline in consumption and investment was most severe in those countries that had accumulated the largest debt imbalances during the pre-crisis credit boom of 2003-07 (Giannone et al., 2011; Lane and Milesi-Ferretti, 2011, 2012, 2014). Finally, the international nature of the crisis also highlights the interdependence across modern financial systems – a crisis that is triggered by an isolated event in one country can quickly

---

4 See, amongst many others, Reinhart and Rogoff (2009), Jorda et al. (2011), Gourinchas and Obstfeld (2012) and Catão and Milesi-Ferretti (2013).

5 McKinsey Global Institute (2010) provides extensive evidence that macroeconomic recovery in the aftermath of financial crises tends to be extremely slow; see also Reinhart and Rogoff (2009).

be transmitted across countries and generate a global crisis through a wide variety of transmission and propagation mechanisms.

In relation to chronic risks, macroeconomic and sectoral performance can be adversely affected by the impact of excessive debt ('debt overhang') on incentives and productive capacity. In the extreme, it is possible to envisage a 'debt Laffer Curve' in which these distortions are so severe that even creditors are made better off by writing down debt to a more sustainable level.

Debt overhang manifests itself in different ways. The evidence indicates that excessive leverage at the corporate and household levels may damage macroeconomic performance (Laeven and Laryea, 2009; Laryea, 2010). While benchmark corporate finance models postulate that financial structures (the split between equity and debt) should have no effect on allocation and production decisions, Myers (1977) demonstrated that the outstanding level of debt can alter the investment decisions of firms.[6] At the household level, debt overhang in the household sector refers to a situation in which over-indebted households forego investments in home improvement or the household supply of labour, while high household debt levels may exert negative macroeconomic effects through the suppression of consumption (Olney, 1999; Mulligan, 2008; Melzer, 2010).

In analogy to corporate debt overhang, debt overhang in the banking sector is a situation in which the scale of the debt liabilities (relative to the value of bank assets) distorts lending decisions, with viable projects not receiving funding since banks seek to scale down balance sheets and reduce debt levels through asset disposals in addition to replenishing capital levels through new equity injections. The adverse implications of systemic deleveraging by the banking system lies behind policy efforts to promote bank recapitalisation, including through publicly funded sources of new capital. The literature on the output losses associated with banking crises is extensive (for recent studies, see Cerra and Saxena, 2008; Furceri and Mourougane, 2009; Reinhart and Rogoff, 2009; Furceri and Zdzienicka, 2012).

In the context of sovereign debt, an excessively high level of public debt may depress economic activity levels through the associated increase in the tax burden and the policy uncertainty associated with ongoing debates about the relative merits of paying the debt versus seeking a debt restructuring. Although the lines of causality are disputed, the empirical evidence also indicates a negative correlation between high levels of public debt and growth performance (Checherita and Rother, 2010; Kumar and Woo, 2010; Reinhart et al., 2012).

Finally, a large external debt generates an array of economic distortions. The classic example is that high external debt acts like a tax on investment, since an expansion in resources will largely be absorbed by increased payments to outstanding creditors (Krugman, 1988; Sachs, 1989). In similar vein, the

---

6   In his framework, debt overhang refers to a situation in which the expected payoff to existing creditors is less than the face value of their claims on the firm. In such a case, the firm must use part of the profits from new investments to pay off existing creditors. Shareholders of limited-liability firms will not internalise this positive 'external' effect of their investment activity and may pass up profitable investment opportunities.

incentive for a government to deliver growth-friendly policies is weakened if domestic residents enjoy only a limited gain from extra output. In addition, a high outstanding level of debt increases fragility in funding markets: the higher level of rollover risk that is associated with a large outstanding stock of debt means that new lenders may be unwilling to provide funds due to the risk of market disruptions. Empirical studies indicate that high external debt is associated with poorer macroeconomic outcomes and greater vulnerability to external crises (Cordella et al., 2005; Imbs and Ranciere, 2008; Reinhart and Rogoff, 2010; Catao and Milesi-Ferretti, 2013).

In addition to the acute and chronic impact of high debt levels, leverage also alters the macroeconomic dynamics in response to various cyclical shocks. In general, the procyclical characteristics of the leverage cycle (rising incomes and asset prices boosting borrowing capacity; declining incomes and asset prices squeezing borrowing capacity) imply that the amplitude and duration of the business cycle are larger compared to those expected in economies without financial frictions. Moreover, leverage also increases the vulnerability of the real economy to financial shocks by affecting the responses of spending levels and productive capacity to shifts in financial conditions. These features have been studied in a range of recent macroeconomic models that study leverage at the household, firm, bank and sovereign levels and at the aggregate level (see, amongst others, Bernanke and Gertler, 1989; Devereux et al., 2006; Mendoza, 2010; Eggertsson and Krugman, 2012; Midrigan and Philippon, 2012; Corsetti et al., 2013; Martin and Philippon, 2014). In Section 3, we provide a stylised framework linking leverage to output dynamics.

Finally, it is important to appreciate how financial globalisation means that cross-border dimensions of leverage are increasingly important. At one level, cross-border funding is an important driver of domestic credit dynamics (Lane and McQuade, 2014). Moreover, the aggregate level of credit in an economy is also determined by direct cross-border lending and bond issuance that bypasses the domestic financial system (Borio et al., 2011). In Section 4, we highlight that the external dimension of debt is especially important for the euro periphery and deficit-running emerging markets.

1.3   Guide to the report

The rest of the report is structured as follows. In Chapter 2, we set the scene by describing the evolution of debt levels around the world; this empirical review is comprehensive in examining sector-level developments as well as aggregate leverage patterns.

Chapter 3 provides some conceptual frameworks that can help guide the interpretation of debt dynamics and the ongoing poisonous interaction between financial crisis and output dynamics. First, we outline the nature of the leverage cycle, a pattern repeated across economies and over time in which a reasonable enthusiasm about economic growth becomes overblown, fostering the belief that there is a greater capacity to take on debt than is actually the case. A financial crisis represents the shock of recognition of this over-borrowing and over-lending, with implications for output very different from a 'normal' recession. Second, we explain the theoretical foundations of debt capacity limits. Debt capacity represents the resources available to fund current and future spending and to repay current outstanding debt. Estimates of debt capacity crucially depend on beliefs about future potential output and can be quite sensitive to revisions in these expectations.

We turn to the case study analysis in Chapter 4. In particular, we (i) address the relevance of the policy response to the leverage crisis in understanding differing macro-financial developments in the US and the Eurozone; and (ii) focus on the risks stemming from the ongoing growth in debt in emerging economies, with a special focus on China and the so-called 'fragile eight'.

Finally, Section 5 discusses some policy implications stemming from our analysis – the lessons from the past crises as well as the policy options currently available to policymakers to manage the legacies of previous crises and to stem the risks, if not the insurgence, of future ones.

2 Global debt analysis: Deleveraging? What deleveraging?

In this chapter, we analyse recent trends in global leverage, focusing on the dynamics of debt-to-income ratios (see Chapter 1 for the motivation behind this). In particular, we consider the evolution of the ratio of total debt to GDP, as well as its components: financials and non-financials, domestic and external, public and private, household and corporate.[7] As shown by recent experience, focusing exclusively on public debt may be misleading; total debt and its composition is what matters for a comprehensive assessment of the leverage problem.

The data point to the following facts:

1. The world is still leveraging up; an overall, global deleveraging process to bring down the total debt-to-GDP ratio – or even to reduce its growth rate – has not yet started. On the contrary, the debt ratio is still rising to all-time highs.

2. In the main Anglo-Saxon economies (namely, the US and the UK), where the deleveraging process in both the financial sector and the household sector has made significant progress, this has come at a cost of increased debt for the consolidated government sector (see Section 4.1).

3. Until 2008, the leveraging up was being led by developed markets, but since then emerging economies (especially China) have been the driving force of the process. This sets up the risk that they could be at the epicentre of the next crisis. Although the level of leverage is higher in developed markets, the speed of the recent leverage process in emerging economies, and especially in Asia, is indeed an increasing concern (see Section 4.3).

4. The level of overall leverage in Japan is off the charts; while its status as a net external creditor is an important source of stability, the sustainability of large sectoral debt levels remains open to question.

Contrary to widely held beliefs, six years on from the beginning of the financial crisis in the advanced economies, the global economy is not yet on a deleveraging path. Indeed, according to our assessment, the ratio of global total debt excluding financials over GDP (we do not have, at this stage, a reliable estimation of financial-sector debt in emerging economies) has kept increasing at an unabated pace and breaking new highs: up 38 percentage points since 2008 to 212%.

---

7   The data appendix at the end of the report explains the definition of variables and the data sources.

Table 2.1   Global debt excluding financials

2013	Total ex-financials a = b + c	Govenment b	Private c	External	Net external position
World	**212**	**78**	**133**	**83**	—
Developed markets	**272**	**108**	**164**	**141**	**-1**
Japan	411	243	168	57	57
Sweden	293	41	252	200	-16
Canada	284	89	195	73	-17
UK	276	90	186	371	-11
US	264	105	160	98	-26
Eurozone	257	93	164	126	-19
Korea	232	37	196	34	-9
Australia	209	29	180	89	-56
Emerging markets	**151**	**48**	**102**	**23**	**-9**
Hungary	223	79	144	148	-103
China	217	49	168	9	18
Czech Republic	131	48	83	56	-51
Poland	137	57	79	73	-71
Thailand	150	45	105	36	-26
Argentina	129	47	82	28	2
South Africa	127	45	82	39	-11
India	120	67	54	23	-25
Brazil	121	66	55	22	-36
Turkey	105	36	69	47	-56
Mexico	77	46	31	32	-40
Indonesia	65	26	39	30	-37
Russia	43	13	29	34	4

Source: Authors' calculation based on OECD, IMF and national accounts data. See Data Appendix at the end of the report. Net external position data are 2012 values.

We can appreciate from both Figure 2.1 (DM denotes developed markets; EM denotes emerging markets) and Table 2.1 that leverage is clearly higher in developed markets (272%) than in emerging markets (151%) – a historic regularity, as shown by Reinhart and Rogoff (2010) amongst others. Moreover, the figure and table show that the increase of the global debt-to-GDP ratio was led by developed markets until 2008 (up 39 percentage points from 2001) and by a sharp acceleration in emerging markets in the post-crisis years (an increase of 36 percentage points, compared with 25 percentage points in developed markets).

Figure 2.1 Global debt excluding financials (% of GDP)

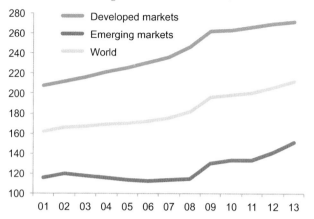

Source: Authors' calculation based on OECD, IMF and national accounts data. See Data Appendix at the end of the report.

In developed markets, for which we also have reliable information on the financial sector, total debt as a percentage of GDP has stabilised since 2010 at a level very close to its all-time high (385%; see Figure 2.2) as a result of a drop in financial-sector leverage, while debt ex-financials has kept rising.

Figure 2.2 Developed markets total debt (% of GDP)

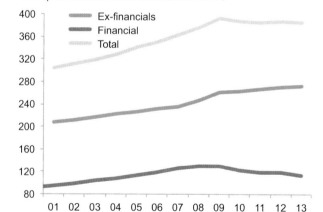

Source: Authors' calculation based on OECD, IMF and national accounts data. See Data Appendix at the end of the report.

Table 2.2 gives a full-blown, granular snapshot of the total debt-to-GDP breakdown for the main developed economies, in all dimensions available.[8] Although direct comparisons of debt levels are difficult because of differences in accounting standards, some key points emerge from the data. Among developed

---

8　Table 2.2 also highlights the particularly difficult situation of the countries belonging to the euro periphery, with both public debt and the net external position at around the 100% threshold (see Chapter 4).

markcts, Japan stands as an outlier, with a total debt of 562% of GDP and debt ex-financials at 411% of GDP. The Eurozone, the UK and the US have broadly similar ratios of debt ex-financials, in the 250-280% range (the UK has a higher total debt due to its larger financial sector relative to GDP), but they have experienced differing dynamics in recent years. Indeed, as shown in Figure 2.3, while leverage ex-financials increased more in the run up from 2001 to 2008 in the UK and the US (+61 and +54 points, respectively) than in the Eurozone (+31 points), since then, due to a combination of a deeper crisis and less efficient policies, leverage has increased slightly more in the Eurozone (+25 points) than in the UK and the US (+23 points and +19 points, respectively).

Turning to emerging markets, it is clear that the driver of the acceleration in the last five years has been China. Indeed, in China the ratio of total debt ex-financials to GDP has increased by a stellar 72 points (Figure 2.3; see section 4.3) to a level that is far higher than in any other emerging economy. Still, leverage has also markedly increased in Turkey (+33 points), Argentina and Thailand.

Looking at the debt breakdown, we can appreciate how the ongoing increase in global leverage is due to both the private and the public debt components. However, even in this regard, there are differences across economies. Indeed, while the upward drift in the ratio of world private debt to GDP until 2008 was driven mainly by developed markets, in the last five years the increase in the global metric has been led by emerging markets (+30 points, to 102%). For the developed markets, there has been some deleveraging in the private sector since 2009, albeit slow and leaving the ratio at elevated levels.

Focusing on developed markets, where we have more granular information and the cross-country information is currently more relevant, we can see that the fall in the private debt-to-GDP ratio was led mainly by the fall in the US and even more so by the UK (-13 and -16 points, respectively, since 2008), where policies have been more successful in this regard. The ratio has remained almost flat in the Eurozone (see Chapters 4 and 5 for a discussion). In particular, the adjustment in the two major Anglo-Saxon economies has concerned households especially, unlike in the Eurozone. In the non-financial corporate sector for developed markets, the leverage ratio has remained more or less flat (Figure 2.3).[9]

Similarly, the US and the UK account for the bulk of the gradual deleveraging process in the financial sector.[10] In the US, the ratio of debt to GDP in the financial sector has in fact fallen to its lowest level since the beginning of the new millennium (again, we will return to this point in Chapter 4). In the UK, however, the leverage of the financial sector remains at very high levels.[11]

Notice that the beginning of private deleveraging in developed markets has come at the cost of an expansion of the government balance sheet. The ratio of

---

[9]   The non-financial corporate debt data for the US are not directly comparable to other countries (since some items are netted out through intra-sectoral consolidation); see also European Central Bank (2012).

[10] The debt of the financial sector is included in the total debt for developed markets that is reported in Figure 2.2, but not in Figure 3.1 and Figures 2.3-2.9. The latter refer to the ex-financials aggregate, which allows us to compute a world aggregate and allows for the developed market (DM) versus emerging market (EM) comparisons.

[11] A large share of the UK financial sector consists of foreign-owned institutions, so the debt of many UK-resident financial firms is ultimately the liability of the parent firms in other parts of world.

Table 2.2 Developed markets debt breakdown

2013	Total a = b+c = d+e	Domestic b	External c	Net external position	Financial d	Total ex-fin. e = f+g	Public f	Private g = h+i	Households h	Non-fin. companies i
DM	**385**	**244**	**141**	**-1**	**113**	**272**	**108**	**164**	**74**	**90**
Japan	562	505	57	57	151	411	243	168	66	102
UK	495	124	371	-11	220	276	90	186	91	94
Sweden	422	223	200	-16	129	293	41	252	85	166
Eurozone	385	259	126	-19	128	257	93	164	64	100
Ireland	1026	10	1016	-116	584	442	124	318	102	216
Netherlands	636	332	304	43	342	294	74	221	126	95
France	347	146	202	-27	93	254	94	161	57	104
Belgium	408	162	246	45	58	350	102	248	56	192
Spain	394	229	166	-95	95	300	94	206	77	129
Portugal	507	276	232	-129	128	379	129	250	87	163
Finland	307	87	220	16	65	242	57	185	66	119
Italy	352	226	127	-34	94	258	133	125	45	81
Greece	317	79	238	-121	13	304	175	129	64	65
Austria	315	119	197	-4	80	235	75	161	53	107
Germany	265	115	150	37	72	193	78	114	57	57
Canada	374	300	73	-17	90	284	89	195	94	101
US	362	264	98	-26	98	264	105	160	79	81
Korea	330	296	34	-9	97	232	37	196	85	110
Australia	298	209	89	-56	89	209	29	180	110	70

Source: Authors' calculations based on OECD, IMF and national accounts data. See Data Appendix at the end of this report.

public debt to GDP in developed markets, almost stable in the decade until 2007, has since then increased by 35 points, reaching well above the 100% threshold.

In particular, this is the other side of the coin of the greater progress made in the private sector in Anglo-Saxon economies. Figure 2.3 shows that the ratio of public debt to GDP increased by 46 points in the UK and by 40 points in the US, which are sharper increases than in the Eurozone (+26 points), since policies in the former countries have (in different ways) permitted a greater expansion of the government balance sheet than in the latter region, so as to allow a gradual deleveraging in the private sector, both financial and non-financial.

Figure 2.3   Global debt breakdown

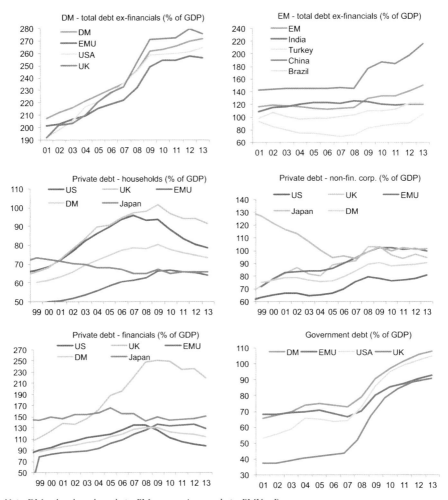

Note: DM = developed markets; EM = emerging markets; EMU = Eurozone.

Source: Authors' calculation based on OECD, IMF and national accounts data. See Data Appendix at the end of the report.

These different balance sheet dynamics between the Eurozone and the US/UK are even more evident when considering central bank balance sheets. Indeed, while during 2008-12 the balance sheets of the Fed and the ECB experienced a similar expansion, since mid-2012 the Fed balance sheet has kept growing under the impulse of QE3, while the ECB balance sheet has been shrinking quite rapidly, along with the reimbursements of the LTROs (see Section 4.2).

3 Leverage cycles and the poisonous combination of rising leverage and slowing growth

The aim of this chapter is to provide some conceptual frameworks that can help guide the interpretation of both debt dynamics and the interaction between financial crises and output dynamics that are studied not only in the global analysis provided in Chapter 2, but also in the case studies depicted in Chapter 4.

In particular, we first outline in Section 3.1 some common properties of leverage cycles, which are described at more length in Appendix 3.A at the end of this chapter, together with the differing effects on output between 'normal' recessions and the various kinds of financial crisis that we identify. Next, in Section 3.2, we review the macroeconomic backdrop of the build-up in debt around the world and the poisonous combination of high and rising global debt and slowing nominal GDP, driven by both slowing real growth and falling inflation. Indeed, the ongoing vicious circle of leverage and policy attempts to deleverage, on the one hand, and slower nominal growth on the other, set the basis for either a slow, painful process of deleveraging or for another crisis, possibly this time originating in emerging economies (with China posing the highest risk). In our view, this makes the world still vulnerable to a further round in the sequence of financial crises that have occurred over the past two decades.

Debt sustainability concerns are elevated by the decline in the level and growth of potential output in both developed and emerging economies relative to when the bulk of the debt was assumed. While there have been long-standing debates about the impact of demographic change and a slower rate of technological progress on potential growth rates, the long-term impact of the 2007-onwards global financial crisis has further contributed to concerns about this slowdown. Appendix 3.B analyses the impact of current and future output growth rates on debt capacity and shows the sensitivity of debt capacity calculations to shifts in the assessment of the level and growth rate of potential output and interest rates.

3.1 Leverage cycles and debt capacity

Among the regularities reported in Reinhart and Rogoff (2009) are distinct differences across types of crises. Some countries repeatedly default on their debt, but others never do. Some countries repeatedly have bouts of high inflation, but others never do. However, whether an economy frequently defaults or never does, or suffers high inflation or keeps it low over time, many countries have banking crises. This suggests that a nation can be largely immunised from sovereign default or high inflation by rule of law or force of precedent. However, financial crises are more about human nature. Laws and regulations set the boundary to credit decisions, but financial innovation, charged by the prospect of capital gain, pushes out that frontier. Finance and leverage advances time and again to breaking point, often with significant consequences for economic activity.

So frequent are these episodes, repeated across regions and over time, that it is possible to offer a stylised description of the cycle of growth enthusiasm, leverage, and bust. In Appendix 3.A, we provide a detailed narrative of a stylised 'leverage cycle' and outline a typology of the different output paths that can be associated with the deleveraging phase that succeeds the end of a lending boom, ranging from a temporary recession to varying degrees of permanently lost output capacity. Of course, each episode is unique so that our schematic will never fit any country episode with precision. Still, understanding the broad sequence of events over time helps to put the past five years into perspective and sets the stage for understanding the next five years. It also helps to identify the policy challenges.

Given the clear macro-financial risks associated with an increase in leverage (as detailed in Chapter 1 and Appendix 3.A, for instance), it is important to understand from an ex ante perspective the factors that can explain rising debt levels. To this end, a key organising framework is the concept of debt capacity, which is the outlined in detail in Appendix 3.B.

3.2   A poisonous combination of high leverage and slower output

The leverage of nations must be put into the perspective of overall economic performance and the composition of borrowing (in terms of currency, maturity, jurisdiction of issuance, and obligator).

In particular, given the definition of leverage that we are examining in this report – the debt-to-GDP ratio – leverage dynamics are intimately related to those of nominal GDP, which in turn is determined by those of both real growth and inflation.

Taking first the dynamics of real growth, Figure 3.1 shows a range of estimates for potential output growth.[12] As shown in the chart, in advanced economies output growth has been on a declining trend for decades, accelerating after the crisis. At a global level, there was an acceleration in real growth from the mid-1990s until the mid-2000s. As made clear by Figure 3.1, this was largely driven by the impressive performance of emerging markets over this period, while the developed economies enjoyed only a temporary improvement in real output growth in the late 1990s which had already started gradually eroding by the mid-2000s. Since the crisis, output growth is estimated to have been declining worldwide.

---

12   We take official estimates from the IMF and OECD. In addition, we extract a time-varying trend from the data by filtering out cyclical fluctuations with the widely-used Hodrick-Prescott statistical filter.

Figure 3.1 Alternative measures of potential real GDP growth

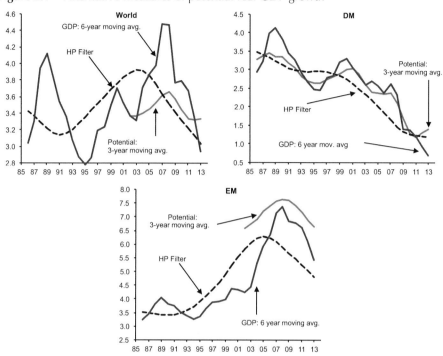

Source: Authors' calculations based on IMF and OECD data. Source for potential output growth is IMF for developed economies and OECD for world aggregate and emerging economies

Potential output growth has not only been declining but has also been subject to downward revisions. These negative revisions to estimates of potential output are illustrated in Figure 3.2, which reports vintages of the IMF staff's forecast in the World Economic Outlook (WEO), in two-year slices from 2008 onwards, for the global aggregate of real GDP growth and the corresponding estimates for the developed and emerging country groups. Each line traces the forecast of the levels of real GDP for the relevant region in various issues of the WEO. Each successive IMF forecast was marked lower, seen as the rotating downwards of the paths of real GDP in the panels for the world, for developed economies, and for emerging economies. To put the markdown of the global aggregate into perspective, the furthest-ahead forecast for the level of real GDP made in 2008, which was for 2012, is currently not expected to be achieved until 2015.

As we explain in detail in Appendix 3.A, these swings in estimates of potential output may be intimately connected to the leverage cycle. In relation to the optimism over growth that prevailed before the crisis, the observed acceleration in growth from the late 1990s until 2007 was supported by the build-up in global debt described in Chapter 2 and at the same time encouraged the increase in leverage in many economies that fed the asset-price and balance-sheet expansion. This expansion phase ultimately came to an end in the financial crisis of 2008-09.

Figure 3.2   IMF GDP forecast vintages (GDP levels, 2006=100)

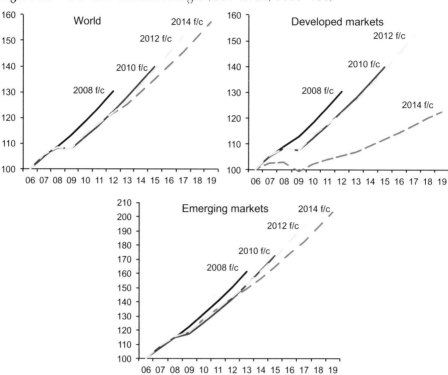

Source: Authors' calculations based on IMF data.

As we show in Appendix 3.A, financial crises may produce not only a persistent drop in the level of output (a 'Type 1' crisis, like in Sweden in the early 1990s), but also a persistent fall in potential output growth (a 'Type 2' crisis, like in Japan since the early 1990s), or a persistent fall in both output and potential output growth (a 'Type 3' crisis). For this reason, the recovery from recessions associated with financial crises can be much slower and follow a different path to that from 'normal' recessions.[13] An important obstacle to recovery from a financial crisis consists of the vicious loop between growth and leverage that occurs in the deleveraging phase, since paying down high debt levels deters activity, with the slowdown in GDP dynamics making the deleveraging process more painful in turn. Accordingly, the leverage cycle amplifies the output cycle, during both the expansion and contraction phases.

Figure 3.3 provides a further perspective on the downgrades to growth projections by comparing the realised levels of real GDP to pre-crisis trend levels. It shows the immediate loss of output during the crisis, the post-crisis persistence of below-trend growth in the developed economies and the interruption to the pre-crisis growth path experienced by emerging economies. According to the patterns shown in Figures 3.1 and 3.3, the advanced economies have endured

---

13   See, amongst many others, Jorda et al. (2013).

a 'Type 3' crisis with a persistent decline in the level and growth rate of output relative to pre-crisis trends, while the emerging economies have experienced what resembles a 'Type 2' crisis in which there is a sustained fall in the growth rate.

Figure 3.3   Real GDP levels (2008=100)

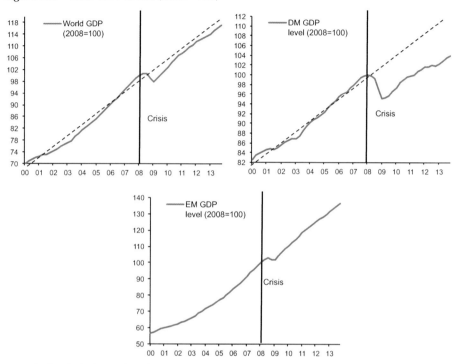

Source: Authors' calculations based on IMF data.

Let us now turn to inflation. Figure 3.4 plots the evolution of consumption-based inflation rates since 2000.[14] The chart shows strong global co-movement of inflation, and points to a worldwide decline since 2011. This decline is particularly strong in advanced economies. A lower-than-expected inflation rate is a worrisome factor for debt sustainability. Since most debt is not indexed to the inflation rate, unexpectedly low inflation constitutes an increase in the real debt burden.[15]

---

14 While there can be important distinctions between the rate of inflation of the GDP deflator and the consumer price index (especially for highly-open economies), we do not dwell on these differences here.

15 Of course, the leverage cycle also acts as a procyclical force in inflation dynamics, through its amplification of aggregate demand fluctuations in both expansion and contraction phases.

Figure 3.4   Inflation rates

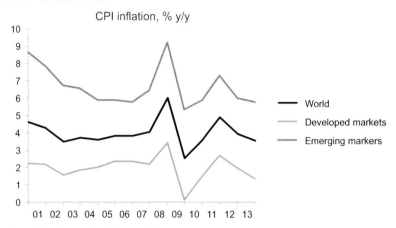

Note: Authors' calculations based on IMF data.

Figures 3.1-3.3 suggest that output growth (and potential output growth) have been declining (albeit to different degrees) in both advanced and developing countries since the crisis. In addition, inflation rates have also failed to rebound after the cyclical downturn during the crisis, such that the path for nominal output growth is substantially lower relative to that expected before the crisis period. If the unexpected decline in inflation persists, an implication is that real interest rates may turn out to be higher than their equilibrium level (which may have declined in line with the decline in potential output growth). Under such conditions, low nominal interest rates in the context of unexpectedly low inflation and declining potential output growth offer little consolation for debt sustainability.

As shown by a weighted (using GDP weights) average of the nominal five-year interest rate, the drop in this representative borrowing rate was smaller than that of nominal GDP growth for emerging markets – and also worldwide – implying increased strain on debt repayment prospects (Figure 3.5). In developed economies instead, yields have declined relative to GDP growth in comparison to the first half of the 2000s (when these economies were leveraging up), with spreads now comparable to the late 1990s. While the fall of nominal yields has helped, the lower bound to nominal interest rates, combined with the unexpected decline in inflation and real growth, raises further concerns about debt sustainability. If, due to an early tightening of monetary policy, nominal yields were to start rising relative to nominal GDP growth, debt dynamics would be negatively affected.

Figure 3.5   Potential nominal GDP growth and nominal yields

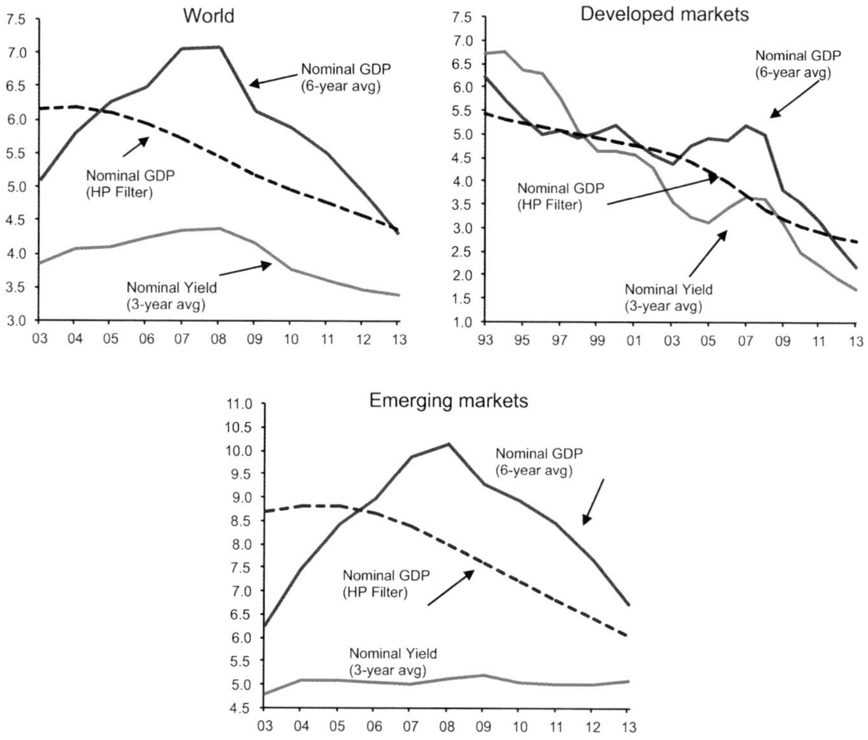

Source: Authors' calculations based on IMF and Haver data.

In summary, as captured in Figure 3.6, the ongoing poisonous combination of high and rising debt documented in Chapter 2 and the slowdown in GDP growth discussed in this section is a source of concern for debt sustainability as well as for any prospect of sustained global recovery. In Chapter 4, against this backdrop, we turn to a detailed analysis of leverage dynamics (and the policy responses) across the US, the Eurozone and emerging economies.

Figure 3.6   Leverage and potential GDP growth

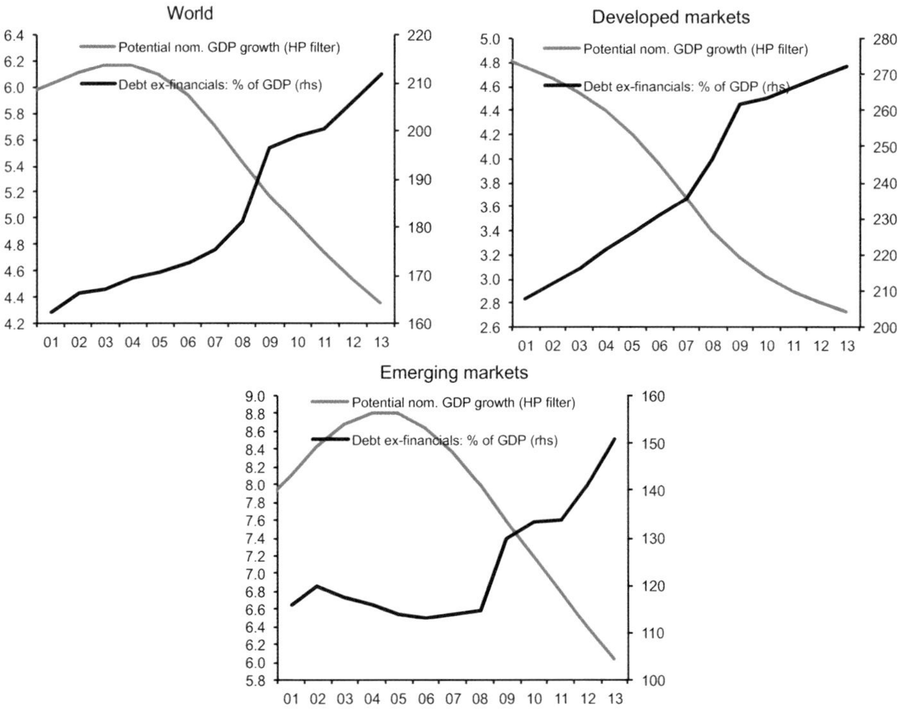

Source: Authors' calculation based on OECD, IMF and national accounts data. See Data Appendix at the end of the report.

Appendix 3A: The leverage cycle

Figure 3A.1 The leverage cycle

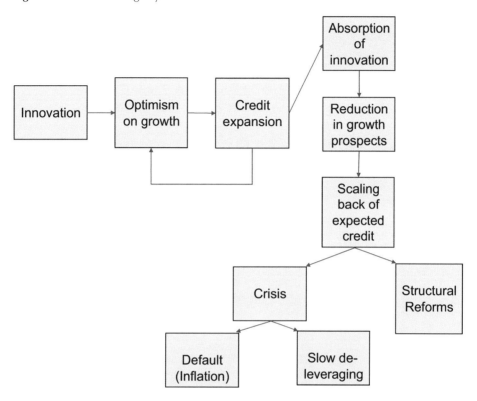

Figure 3A.1 lays out the sequence of events associated with the leverage cycle. Each box marks a distinct episode in the cycle. An episode typically begins with an innovation that resets the landscape, whether a technological breakthrough that advances the production function, a financial innovation that creates a new instrument or opens markets, or a distinct change in the legal regime. Prior technological innovations include the invention of the diving bell, the canal building boom, the great expansion of railroads, the routinised refrigeration of beef that opened the Pampas of Argentina, the advent of radio, the widespread adoption of television, and that improvements in fibre optics that made the internet scalable. Financial innovation over the ages included the recognition that the tulip bulb could be a store of value, that notes on the government could be tradable (as in the South Sea Bubble), that equity in homes could be unlocked, or that individual claims could be pooled and their income flows tiered in such a way to meet the needs of different investors.[16] Legal changes altered the landscape of finance with the opening of capital accounts across many economies from the

---

16   Kindleberger and Aliber (2011) is the classic reference on this topic. On tulips, see also Dash (2009).

1960s to 1980s and the accession of important economies to the WTO, notably shaping the Chinese experience of the past decade.

These innovations directly spur aggregate supply, certainly its level and often its rate of growth. Thus, as in the transition to the next box, innovation is followed by optimism over economic prospects. When households, firms and the government collectively embrace taking on more debt because they think they can, they do. Indeed, many economic models explain the rationality of borrowing in anticipation of future increases in income. After all, people can pull future income forward through borrowing to consume today, confident that they have the wherewithal to service that debt out of higher future incomes. Thus, optimism over economic growth feeds directly into credit expansion, as in the transition of the boxes. Essentially, the expectation of a higher track of potential output leads people to mark up their expected capacity to take on debt.

Often, in the last half-century or so, the world 'miracle' has been used to highlight periods of high growth initially spurred by genuine innovations and then sustained by increased borrowing: from the 'Italian miracle' to the 'Latin America miracle', the 'Japanese miracle', the 'South-East Asia miracle', the 'US miracle', the 'Irish miracle', the 'Spanish miracle' and last, but not least, the 'Chinese miracle'. By now we know how these 'miracles' have ended: in various forms of financial crisis when the 'irrational exuberance' of leverage went beyond repayment capacity after the positive supply-side shocks spurred by innovation faded. (Our judgment on China is still suspended, although the risks are rising as we show in Section 4.3).

The problem is that curbing newfound enthusiasm about future prospects for income may prove disruptive for overall macroeconomic performance. Leverage can be used to prolong the dreams spurred by the 'miracle', with the idea that the debt capacity is still there. In Italy, when the raw materials shocks of 1971 and 1973 halted the post-war miracle, leveraging of the public sector rather than supply-side reforms was used as a weapon to fight the trend. The resulting higher debt stock did not precipitate an explicit default crisis, but at times it was a close-run thing. Instead, there was a slow and silent crisis in which the incentives to inflate away the problem rose and policymakers embarked on a series of deleveraging attempts. As a consequence of sluggish growth for more than two decades, the ratio of public debt to GDP persistently remained above 100%.

In the late 1970s, recycling 'petro dollars' fuelled Latin American economies. Cash-flush oil producers put their wealth to work by lending to Latin American sovereigns through the intermediation of US money centre banks, providing a higher return than elsewhere and sparking a leap forward in development on the back of massive capital investment. What ensued was the debt crisis of 1981-82 and a decade of sluggish expansion in the region.

In the mid-1990s, authorities in the 'miracle-growth' countries of East Asia explained that their success owed to 'Asian values' and argued that financial crises were a purely Latin American phenomenon. The crisis of 1997-1998 changed that tune.

Soothing words were similarly spoken by senior US officials in 2006 as they basked in the glow of the Great Moderation, as economists called the damping of business-cycle fluctuations over the prior two decades. Financial institutions were rock solid and lean, not leveraged. Financial markets were resilient. And housing prices never declined on a nationwide basis.

The key reinforcing mechanism of growth and leverage is seen as the circular arrow in the flow chart. People borrow more when they believe their incomes will expand. This borrowing directly fuels demand, providing the self-justifying evidence that income prospects are indeed higher; de facto it blurs, and inflates, estimates of potential output. And, for a time, aggregate supply may be rising faster than the prior norm, depending on the underlying innovation and the stage of its absorption into the productive process.

As Paul David's research points out, the absorption of a technological advance follows an S-shaped curve: slow at first, faster as the new technique spreads through the economy and other aspects of factory work adapt to it, and then slow again as diminishing returns set in (David, 1989). Credit expansion disguises, for a time, the second bend to the S. Only over time does the slowing in growth prospects become evident. On that realisation, it becomes necessary to shift the entire path of expected future income lower. At that point, the nation's debt capacity, or the present value of all future income, is marked lower. Correspondingly, there is a scaling back of expectations about the amount of credit that is sustainable on balance sheets.

Figure 3A.2 Alternative scenarios for recognition of excessive optimism

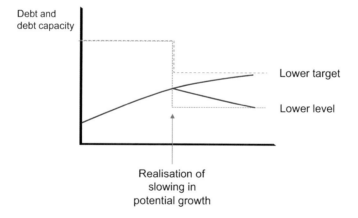

The key question for adjustment is: How far do expectations about future debt capacity fall? Figure 3A.2 offers two stark alternative scenarios for the recognition of excessive optimism. The difference between the two scenarios revolves around whether the reduction in debt capacity binds future plans or the current level of debt. In the relatively more benign (or less malign) case, marked-down growth prospects imply that a nation cannot accumulate as much debt as planned before the recognition that its optimism was excessive. A lower debt capacity therefore implies a lower target for future debt, which can be accomplished by slowing the pace of the accumulation of additional debt over time.

Much more bracing to economic prospects is a reduction in debt capacity to below current debt levels. The recognition of excessive optimism triggers the understanding that the nation has already over-borrowed relative to its capacity to repay. To live within the limit of this lower level of debt capacity, borrowing has to contract, representing a more significant headwind to continued economic expansion.

The different potential outcomes once excessive optimism is recognised explain why the tree diagram in Figure 3A.1 subsequently branches out. The shock that current debt levels cannot be supported by future growth in potential output is more likely to be associated with a crisis, as the level of the debt has to be paid down or its accumulation slowed down abruptly, either overall or in some of its key components – private borrowing from banks, public debt, foreign debt – either explicitly, via defaults, or implicitly, via inflation.

Even a relatively smooth slowing of the pace of additional borrowing, the middle branch, involving a gradual grind of deleveraging, is harmful to economic performance because of the growth and debt nexus. However, it is likely to be more manageable given the appropriate policy response.

The rightmost branch is the aspiration of most politicians. A government overburdened by debt could, in principle, launch structural reforms to expand productive potential. This is the historical rationale for the pairing of additional lines of credit in programmes of the International Monetary Fund with promises of structural adjustment, such as reducing monopoly concentration, reforming the tax system, and opening up to foreign trade.

The attributes of debt outstanding and a nation's ongoing access to borrowing shape the path of adjustment. There are four important attributes of debt that influence the form of deleveraging. All else equal, an economy is better positioned to weather a ratcheting down of its debt capacity when its outstanding obligations are (i) of long maturity; (ii) denominated in its own currency over which it has the ability to print; (iii) issued in its own jurisdiction; and (iv) owned by non-residents who have little sway over the political process.

The need to readjust to a lower debt capacity is associated with some economic dislocations. Three alternative scenarios for the path of real GDP over time, corresponding to the three branches of the tree diagram, are provided in Figure 3A.3.

Figure 3A.3 Alternative scenarios for real GDP

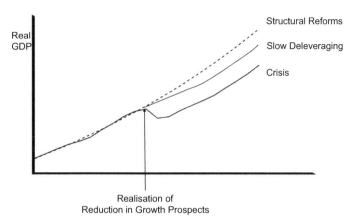

The dotted line corresponds to when structural reforms make it possible for the economy to grow its way out of the problem of excess debt by tilting up the path of potential output. However, structural reforms seldom have an immediate payoff, especially when they are significant in size and unanticipated. For instance, an improvement in competitiveness – through a compression in domestic prices and costs – may help on the trade front, but it also lowers nominal GDP, thereby increasing the burden of debt.

The 'slow deleveraging' is less dramatic but its toll on the economy accumulates over time. Essentially, the middle path is a crisis stretched out as output expands only sluggishly, at best, as the need to cut borrowing imposes significant headwinds. Over time, there is a permanent output loss in light of the decrease in physical and human capital stock as fixed investment is held back and high unemployment damages skills.

The third scenario corresponds to a wrenching adjustment of output. Reinhart and Reinhart (2010) look at the 15 worst financial crises of the second half of the 20th century. In the median experience, the level of real GDP per capita ten years after the crisis is 15% below the level predicted by the trend extrapolated from the ten years prior to the crisis. A crisis is costly.

Figure 3A.3 depicting the three scenarios is just a stylised description. A financial crisis influences both aggregate demand (the business cycle) and aggregate supply (the secular trend), depending on its origin, the composition of debt, and the policy response. In that regard, it is useful to recall that a crisis is very different from a recession. A recession produces a temporary loss of output followed by a rebound of growth above that of its potential so as to recover to the trend path prevailing before the recession (left panel of Figure 3A.4). As is illustrated by the right panel of Figure 3A.4, a good example is the recession experienced by the US in 1982.

Figure 3A.4 Recession, but not a crisis

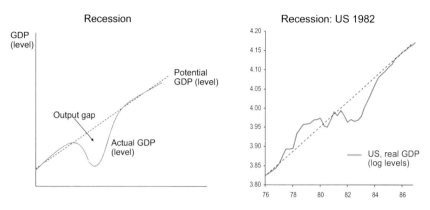

In a crisis, the loss of output or the slowdown in output growth is not temporary, but persistent. Indeed, with this background, we can classify three different paths for an economy depending on whether the hit stemming from a crisis is to the level or to the growth rate of potential output, or both. These paths essentially differ as to the mix of policies in response to the wealth loss created by the crisis. Officials need to deal with the direct effects on spending – demand management – and the underlying financial policies that made the crisis possible – structural reform.

(i) Type 1 crisis: Permanent loss of output, but potential growth unchanged

Figure 3A.5 Type 1 crisis: Persistent output loss

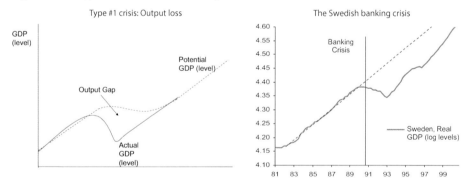

A Type 1 financial crisis is one in which, unlike a recession, the level of output shows a persistent loss, but potential output growth remains unchanged. That is, the economy, after having contracted for one or more years, resumes growing at the prior growth rate. Unlike in a recession, the following recovery is not above-trend. As a consequence, the output loss is persistent relative to the trend of output before the crisis. A typical case of a pre-2008 Type 1 crisis is the Swedish banking crisis of the early 1990s. Although the output loss was never recovered relative to the trend before the crisis, the economy started to grow again at a pace similar to the pre-crisis rate (thanks to an appropriate set of crisis-management policies).

(ii) Type 2 crisis: Persistent fall in output growth

Figure 3A.6 Type 2 crisis

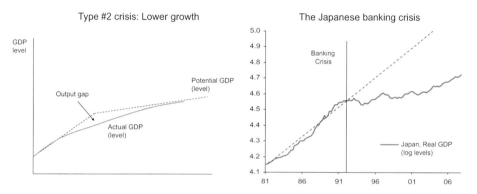

A Type 2 financial crisis is one in which the level of output does not contract in any meaningful way, perhaps because bankruptcies or defaults are not allowed and public debt inflates. However, due to the extent of the problems or to wrong policies (lack of bank recapitalisation, monetary policy not sufficiently expansionary, etc.), a steep pace of deleveraging in some sectors of the economy (bank lending, external financing, etc.) spreads over a long period of time, so that potential output growth slows down in a permanent way. A Type 2 crisis could easily be more disruptive than a Type 1 crisis despite a lack of systemic bankruptcies and output contraction, since erroneous policies can make the crisis much more persistent. A typical pre-2008 case of a Type 2 crisis was the Japanese banking crisis of the early 1990s (panel B of Figure 3A.6). Although output never contracted in any meaningful way relative to, say, the Swedish banking crisis, the pace of potential growth of the Japanese economy never reverted to the pre-crisis rate (due to a combination of wrong policies and supply-side factors, such as demographics). In just a few years from the beginning of the crisis, the output loss relative to the pre-crisis trend was much greater than in Sweden. Moreover, the overall economy never delevered, as public debt ballooned. The risks of a dramatic default, either explicit or implicit, remain.

(iii) Type 3 Crisis: Loss of output and slower potential output growth

As illustrated in Panel A of Figure 3A.7, the worst type of financial crisis is one in which both the level and the growth rate of potential output are affected sizeably and negatively, due to both the roots of the crisis and the policy response.

The post-2008 crisis that occurred in developed markets has turned out to be a Type 3 crisis since it has been characterised by a persistent loss of output and, arguably, a slowdown in the trend global growth rate. A glance at the profile of developed-market GDP is quite indicative of the fact that what occurred after 2007 was a debt crisis rather than a recession: the 5% output loss until Q1 2009 was persistent (panel B of Figure 3A.7) and the loss actually widened relative to what could be considered as the trend prevailing until 2007, as growth slowed significantly (Figure 3.1).

Figure 3A.7 Type 3 crisis

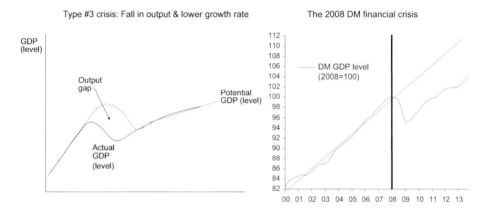

Appendix 3B: Debt capacity

In the case of any debt contracted in terms of money (as opposed to indexed to the prices of another currency, a good, or a basket of goods and services), it is the path of nominal income that is relevant for debt sustainability. If real income is lower than when the debt was incurred, repayment will take a larger-than-expected share of real resources. If inflation runs slower than anticipated, the real rate on debt will be higher than the borrower expected, again implying that repayment requires a larger-than-expected share of real resources.

The nature of the leverage cycle is that, at least initially, mistakes in estimating debt capacity are self-reinforcing. That is, debt fuels demand that pushes up top-line growth, seeming to justify debt accumulation. Given the clear macro-financial risks associated with an increase in leverage as detailed in Section 1, it is important to understand from an ex ante perspective the factors that can explain rising debt levels and where there is scope for mistakes. To this end, it is useful to focus on the debt capacity of nations, or the resources available to fund current and future spending and to repay current debt outstanding.

For an economy, the limit to consumption is determined by the time path of its potential to produce output. In particular, if potential output in year *t* in economy j is denoted as $Y_{j,t}^p$, then the net present value of future output in real terms, or the discounted sum of all future income, $NPV_{j,t}$ is given as:

$$NPV_{j,t} = \sum_{i=0}^{\infty} \frac{Y_{j,t+i}^P}{(1+\rho_j)^i}$$

where ρ is some constant discount rate to be specified later.[17] It is convenient to express the future path of potential output as the product of the current level and compounded future growth rates. If the growth rate is assumed to be constant at σ_j, then we have:

$$NPV_{j,t} = Y_{j,t}^P \sum_{i=0}^{\infty} \left[\frac{1+\sigma_j}{1+\rho_j}\right]^i$$

In turn, this simplifies to:

$$NPV_{j,t} = Y_{j,t}^P \frac{1}{\rho_j - \sigma_j}$$

This framework suggests three opportunities to set off a leverage cycle as debt capacity turns out to be less ample than anticipated when new debt was accumulated. Because the calculation of debt capacity involves a ratio, the mistake could be in the numerator (the right level of output at which to start the path) or the denominator (expected growth or the appropriate discount rate).

Three types of expectation errors are illustrated by Greece, Ireland and Italy. According to IMF estimates, Greek real GDP was 10% above its potential level by 2008. Since this was not sufficiently recognised at the time (contemporaneous estimates of potential output were more optimistic), these dynamics opened up the possibility that borrowers might misinterpret an overstretched economy as a new standard of sustainable output, and take on excessive debt.

Revisions to the denominator have a more dramatic impact. Ireland is the advanced economy for which the IMF's estimate of potential output growth moved within the widest range. In the mid-1980s, the Irish economy was expected to expand at a sub 2% pace. By 1998, the estimate of secular growth had breached 9%. Robust estimates followed for a time, but then the assessment turned markedly lower, declining by about one percentage point every year starting in 2000, and bottoming at net contractions in potential output from 2009 to 2011. These sharp swings in growth prospects followed through to even sharper movements in the nation's ability to take on debt in real terms through the extrapolation of current potential output growth estimates in estimating the present value of future income streams.

---

17 Assuming a constant discount rate may be giving the game away at the outset. Cochrane (2011) argues that time variation in the discount rate is critical in understanding asset prices.

The other element of the denominator of the debt-capacity calculation is the discount rate. Within the last 20 years, the premium on Italian over German debt went from almost 5 percentage points to 20 basis points and nearly back again, before falling to about 150 basis points. If the discount rate on future income were to vary in that same range, the changes in the private sector's assessment of debt capacity would be sizable. Over the last 15 years, the accession of Italy to the Eurozone compressed this spread, which, if extrapolated as a decline in the discount rate, sharply raised debt capacity. What markets give they sometimes take back, and the subsequent spread-widening resulted in a wrenching contraction in the net present value of future output. The consequences for the ability to manage debt in the transition are self-evident.

4 Case studies

4.1 The United States

4.1.1 The re-leveraging of the US economy

The role of debt accumulation in the US in the run-up to the financial crisis of 2008 is best seen in a longer perspective. The Federal Reserve's Financial Accounts (formerly Flow of Funds) provides a comprehensive look into the balance sheets of US households, businesses and government. As shown in Figure 4.1, there have been two peaks in aggregate debt relative to nominal GDP over the past century. The first, in 1932-1933, epitomises the process of Fisherian debt-deflation.[18] The ratio of debt to nominal GDP spiked sharply because nominal GDP collapsed under the weight of sizable declines in both prices and quantities. As a consequence, all the components of debt in the layer chart moved higher.

Figure 4.1   US total debt by sector (% of GDP)

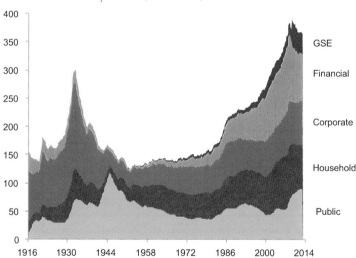

Source: Authors' calculations based on national accounts data.

The expansion in debt to its next peak at the beginning of 2008 was more gradual and built upon increases in the numerator, not declines in the denominator.

---

18   This was identified in real time in Fisher (1933).

Moreover, it was a private-sector phenomenon, as net government obligations in relation to nominal GDP moved sideways after the step-up propelled by the Bush tax cuts. The speed of the ascent is striking. In the five years after 2003, the ratio of total debt to GDP rose 62 percentage points, led by a 22 percentage point increase in the debt share of the financial sector and a 12 percentage point increase by households.

The pullback since has been uneven and in the aggregate pales in significance compared to the earlier rise, even if there has been more adjustment than in other regions (such as the Eurozone). To be sure, the financial sector trimmed its sails with both write-downs and goading from supervisors and regulators, resulting in a decline in the sector's debt-to-GDP ratio by about 37 percentage points. Households and, to a lesser extent, state and local governments also delevered, with their GDP shares falling 17 percentage points and 2 percentage points, respectively. Contrary to the widespread perception and self-congratulations of public officials, the US remains highly levered today as a consequence of a near 38 percentage point increase in federal debt relative to nominal GDP. In addition to the growing federal deficit, the bailouts of the government-sponsored enterprises (GSEs), AIG and the auto industry propelled the 50 percentage point increase in total public debt relative to GDP.[19]

The role of the leverage cycle — its surge of self-fulfilling enthusiasm followed by despair — is seen best in Figure 4.2. The solid line plots the level of US real GDP per capita in international dollars, while the dashed line plots the level of real GDP per capita extrapolated from the ten-year trend ending in 2001. There are two sources of difference between the solid and dashed lines corresponding to the overestimate of the trend and the lack of recognition of the cyclical position of the economy. In fact, output was close to its prior trend through 2007, but the estimated level of potential output was below both trend and actual GDP. That is, the encouragement to leverage associated with the belief that a high trend would continue forever pushed aggregate demand into the excess zone. For a time, headline growth supported that belief even as the foundation to it was undermined by a slowing in the growth of potential output. Debt taken on prior to 2007 might have seemed manageable at the time, but that was not the outcome in the event.

---

19   The increase in GSE debt is due to accounting for mortgage pools differently after the move of the two housing-related entities into government conservatorship in 2008.

Figure 4.2   US output, actual and past trends

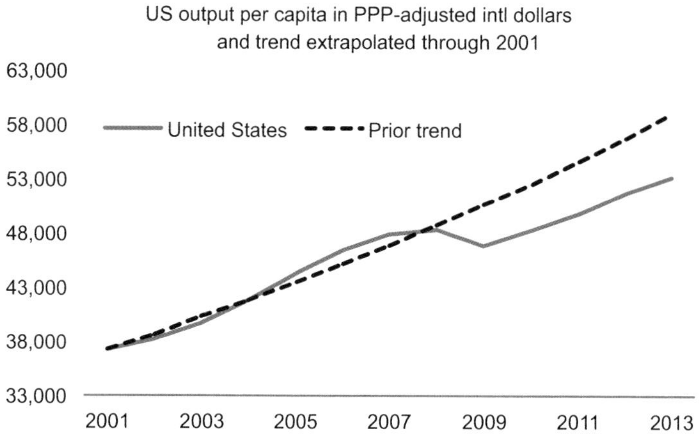

US output per capita in PPP-adjusted intl dollars
and trend extrapolated through 2001

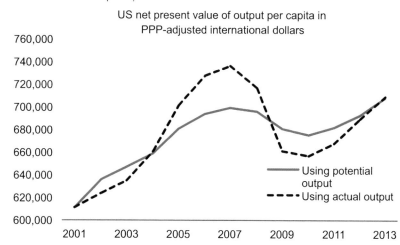

Source: IMF (2014b), authors' calculations.

This over-enthusiasm is seen more starkly in debt capacity (Figure 4.3). The solid line calculates the net present value of future output launching from the then-current estimate of potential output. The dashed line starts the net present value summation from the current level of output. Borrowers looking at their current incomes in the early 2000s might not have appreciated that the then-apparent debt capacity was unsustainable because excess demand was untenable and growth would slow. The sharp break in the dashed line makes it plain that debtors would be pressed to repay.

Figure 4.3   US debt capacity

US net present value of output per capita in
PPP-adjusted international dollars

Source: IMF (2014b), authors' calculations.

The official policy response to an untenable ratio of debt to income economy-wide followed multiple avenues. First, as already noted, the private sector was encouraged to deal with unsustainable obligations through stress tests of large financial intermediaries. Second, some of those obligations were directly lifted from the private to the public sector balance sheet, notably including the conservatorship of the housing-related GSEs and aid in the bankruptcy of major auto companies.

Some of the balance sheet relief came from the policy of the Federal Reserve, above and beyond keeping the federal funds rate pinned to its zero lower bound. Aside from its temporary operations, the Fed acquired private sector obligations through its Maiden Lane facilities and bought outright debt of agencies, their guaranteed mortgage-backed securities, and Treasury securities. The net result is evident in Figure 4.4, which scales the aggregate size of the Fed's balance sheet to nominal GDP since 1918, which now rises to a quarter of annual nominal output.

Figure 4.4   Federal Reserve balance sheet (% of GDP)

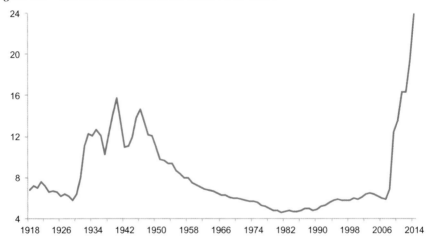

Source: Authors' calculations based on Federal Reserve data.

At this juncture, official efforts in the US can be credited with turning the path of output decidedly upwards, and more so than in other advanced economies. Harder to judge are the latent risks. Will the high level of federal debt pose a problem down the road (especially as it interacts with the budget consequences of decidedly adverse demographics and the realignment of Fed policy)? Will the Fed come to realign its balance sheet in time to avoid a significant increase in the price level and perhaps acceleration thereafter, while recognising that this will be occurring against the backdrop of a sizeable accumulation of wealth in the private sector and signs of increased leverage (a subject to consider in somewhat more depth)? In Chapter 5, we briefly discuss these policy challenges.

As for wealth, as shown in Table 4.1, the increase in household assets from 2008 to 2013 matches that in the five-year lead-up to the crisis and is double the valuation loss in the distress period. Liabilities have declined in total, paced by a reduction in home mortgages. Stock market gains have provided the largest boost to assets, while on the liability side very low interest rates have boosted demand for auto loans, and educational aspirations have driven strong gains in student loans.

Table 4.1 US households' balance sheet

$, billions	Level		Change	
	2013	**2002-07**	**2007-08**	**2008-13**
Assets				
Total assets	94,042	29,394	-10,750	22,566
Real estate at market value	22,070	7,095	-3,524	2,208
Consumer durable goods	5,011	949	103	432
Total financial assets	66,498	21,238	-7,355	19,836
Liabilities				
Total liabilities	13,768	5,636	-116	-510
Home mortgages	9,386	4,583	-32	-1,193
Consumer credit	3,097	619	35	447
Net worth	80,274	23,758	-10,634	23,076

Source: Authors' calculations based on Federal Reserve and national accounts data.

Ongoing monetary policy accommodation has made it easier for households to carry their debt loads. With the nominal short-term interest rate pinned to its zero lower bound, the interest cost associated with this debt is at a very low level. As shown in Figure 4.5, a concise way to illustrate this is the household financial obligation ratio – a broad measure of estimated required payments on outstanding mortgages, consumer debt, auto leases, home rental payments, insurance and property tax. This ratio of debt to disposable income has declined from a peak of 18.1 in 2007:Q4 to 15.4 in 2013:Q4, indicating that households are better able to keep up with debt payments, as long as Federal Reserve policy accommodation stays in place. Note that much of this household debt is of short maturity or taken down with adjustable rates. When the time comes for the Fed to renormalise its policy rate, however, these ratios will head north, potentially putting strains on some households.

Figure 4.5   Household debt-carrying costs (% of disposable income)

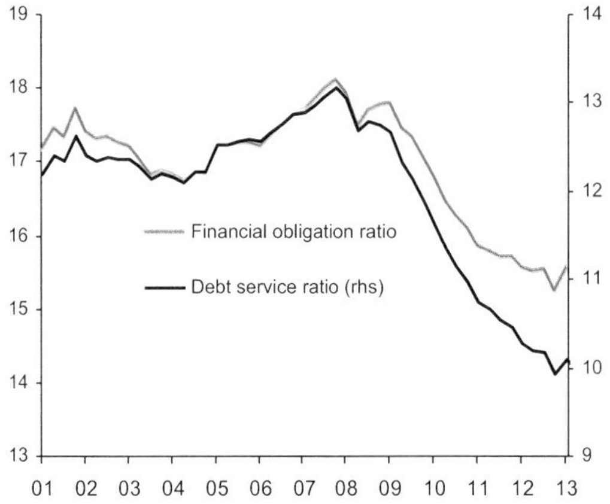

Source: Authors' calculations based on Federal Reserve data.

Unlike households and financials, the US non-financial corporate sector has already re-levered, as these firms have taken advantage of the long period of low interest rates to issue bonds and take on new, orrefinance existing, obligations. Indeed, loan and short-term market obligations are roughly at their level of the early 1990s. This lending has mostly been about finance, not real activity. Firms have built up cash buffers, increased dividends, and bought back stock. Spending on fixed investment has actually been quite subdued. For now, net interest payments remain low in light of the Federal Reserve's policy accommodation. As opposed to that of households, the debt of non-financial firms tends to have a longer maturity, lengthening the runway before interest costs take off substantially when the Fed begins to tighten.

What raises worries about over-borrowing in the private sector is the other side of the transactions –over-lending by investors. For six years, the Federal Reserve has kept the short-term interest rate low and purchased long-duration Treasury securities and convex mortgage-backed securities. This is a direct encouragement to investors to stretch for yield in alternative, often less familiar, markets. In effect, the Fed has been 'recruiting' investors to purchase risky assets (Stein, 2012). The problem is that not all investors may appreciate the extent of the risk they acquire in the bargain. This suggests that focusing solely on economy-wide aggregate quantities is not sufficient to appreciate potential system risks associated with the re-leveraging of the US economy. Monitoring also has to encompass asset prices, risk spreads and activity in specific market niches.

Indeed, across the world there is considerable heterogeneity in the sensitivity of aggregate demand to housing. There are several reasons to suspect that it is on the high side in the US: housing tends to make up a higher share of household wealth; home ownership is higher than in most other countries and reaches further down the income distribution; and non-recourse, long-term, fixed-rate mortgages provide an effective mechanism to tap equity. But perhaps most importantly, homes represent a key source of collateral, sometimes embedded in complicated ways in housing finance. As detailed in Mian and Sufi (2014), disruptions in collateral chains have powerful influences on economic activity.

This narrative points to an important role for housing and asset prices in the balance sheet of the private sector and suggests that the post-crisis deleveraging process has been particularly powerful because of the collapse of these prices. In what follows, we propose a quantitative exercise designed to identify those changes in sectoral balance sheets and saving behaviour since the crisis that have been 'exceptionally' large. By exceptionally large, we mean changes that go beyond what can be explained by the large drop in nominal GDP observed since 2008.

The last recession was particularly severe by historical standards; according to NBER recession dating, the deepest and longest in our sample (1983-2013). Developments so far suggest that it corresponded to what we have labelled a 'crisis' rather than a classical recession (see Appendix 3.A). Not only was the output contraction severe and the recovery slow, but associated with the recession, we have also seen a banking crisis and a collapse of asset prices. As has been documented extensively, recessions and banking crises do not always coincide, but when they do the balance sheet adjustment following the crisis is more severe (Reinhart and Rogoff, 2009; Jorda et al., 2013).

To what extent has the US deleveraging process observed since the crisis been exceptionally severe in the sense defined above? One way to provide a quantitative answer to this question is through counterfactual analysis. In what follows, we propose a counterfactual experiment based on a model including a rich set of macroeconomic and balance sheet variables.

4.1.2 The counterfactual scenario

We consider 18 variables, including indicators of the real economy, nominal and interest rate variables, housing prices and residential investment, savings by sector as well as debt variables for households, financial and non-financial corporations (see Table 4.2 for a description).

The counterfactual is constructed from the estimation of a large dynamic model (see Box 4.1 for details) including all variables described in Table 4.2.

Table 4.2 Data description

Variable	Description	Source	Transformation
IR 10y	10-Year Treasury Constant Maturity Rate	Federal Reserve Board	-
IR 3m	3-Month Treasury Bill: Secondary Market Rate	Federal Reserve Board	-
Consumption	Personal Consumption Expenditures	Bureau of Economic Analysis	Log
Employment	All Employees: Total nonfarm	Bureau of Labor Statistics	Log
S&L Gov Saving	Gross government saving: State and local	Bureau of Economic Analysis	-
Real GDP	Gross Domestic Product	Bureau of Economic Analysis	Log
Fed Gov Saving	Gross Government Saving	Bureau of Economic Analysis	-
NR Priv Inv	Private Nonresidential Fixed Investment	Bureau of Economic Analysis	Log
R Priv Inv	Private Residential Fixed Investment	Bureau of Economic Analysis	Log
HH Debt/PI	Household Debt Service Payments as a Percent of Disposable Personal Income	Federal Reserve Board	-
House Prices	All-Transactions House Price Index for the United States	Federal Housing Finance Agency	Log
HH Savings	Gross private saving: Households and institutions	Bureau of Economic Analysis	Log
HH Credit Liab	Households and Nonprofit Organizations; Credit Market Instruments; Liability, Level	Federal Reserve Board	Log
NFC Credit Liab	Nonfinancial Corporate Business; Credit Market Instruments; Liability	Federal Reserve Board	Log
Fin Bus Credit Liab	Financial Business; Credit Market Instruments; Liability, Level	Federal Reserve Board	Log
CPI	Consumer Price Index for All Urban Consumers: All Items	Bureau of Labor Statistics	Log
SP 500	S&P 500 Stock Price Index	S&P Dow Jones Indices LLC	Log
HH Assets/PI	Households and nonprofit organizations; total assets / Disposable Personal Income	Federal Reserve Board; U.S. Department of Commerce: Bureau of Economic Analysis	-

Given the parameter estimates, this counterfactual is computed as conditional forecasts of the variables of interest included in the model, where the conditioning information is given by: (i) the 1983:Q1-2007:Q4 history of all variables in the model; and (ii) the observed outcomes of the level of real GDP and CPI until the end of the sample in 2013:Q3. Box 4.1 reports technical details.

Figure 4.6 reports the 2.5% and 97.5% percentiles of the counterfactual forecast distributions, as a measure of the width of the distributions. Any developments outside those percentiles are identified as being 'unlikely' or 'exceptional', given the historical regularities our model identifies in the pre-crisis data and the business cycle paths that we have defined.

Figure 4.6 Conditional forecast – recession 2007-08

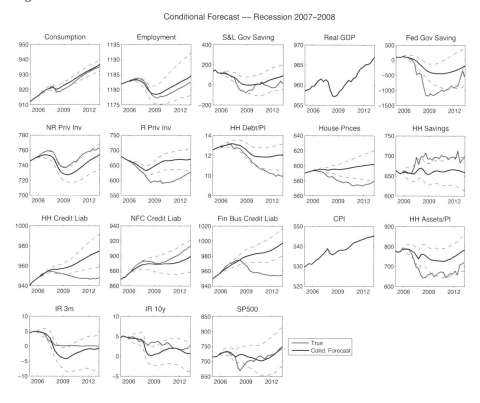

Conditional Forecast –– Recession 2007–2008

Some of the variables considered show no significant difference between the counterfactual and the realised paths (both paths are within the bands of the counterfactual distribution). These are all the macroeconomic variables, stock prices (with the exception of 2008) and the liabilities of non-financial corporations. Notwithstanding their volatility since the crisis, their dynamics are not 'exceptional' in the sense that they correspond to their historical association with nominal GDP. This is not the case for variables related to housing (non-residential investment and housing prices), variables related to household net worth (the ratio of household assets to personal income, household liabilities, the ratio of household debt service payments to disposable income), variables related to the fiscal stance (government savings during the recession years), the liabilities of financial businesses, and nominal interest rates until late 2011.

According to our metric of what constitutes an 'exceptional adjustment', there is a clear difference between household and financial institutions on one hand, and non-financial corporations on the other. While the former sectors have engaged in a sharp and 'exceptional' deleveraging process, the latter has not. Household deleveraging has taken place in association with an exceptional decline in the asset-to-income ratio, housing prices and residential investment. Household deleveraging has also been associated with (and possibly made possible by) an unusually aggressive fiscal policy stance in 2009-10 (as shown by the path of public saving in the chart) which is matched by an 'exceptional' increase in private saving. Interestingly, the exceptional deleveraging of the financial sector has not implied an exceptional deleveraging of non-financial corporations, which have behaved in line with their past correlation with business cycle dynamics. Monetary policy, although it has been very aggressive, was constrained by the zero lower bound for a few years after the crisis, which is clearly shown by the fact that the counterfactual path of the three-month interest rate has been below zero. The results also suggest that quantitative easing in 2009-10 was more effective in supporting stock prices. The quick rebound in stock prices is likely to be the explanation for the recovery of household assets relative to personal income.

An interpretation of these findings is that the exceptional deleveraging of households has been associated with a shock to the value of assets, driven by a collapse in housing prices, and cannot be explained solely by the shock on income. We elaborate more on this point in the next sub-section, when we compare the US and the Eurozone cases. Facing that, policy has been supportive of the process of adjustment – via income through the fiscal tool, and via asset prices through quantitative easing.

Clearly, the output shock, and even its persistence, cannot alone explain the deleveraging process of households and the financial sector since the crisis. Specific features of the last crisis, such as the pre-crisis high level of debt and the exceptional collapse of housing prices affecting the value of household assets, are a big part of the story.

Box 4.1

The model

Let X_t be the vector including the n variables (all variables are in log-levels, except for variables expressed in rates or with negative levels that are in levels). We estimate a VAR model with p (=4) lags:
$$X_t = A_0 + A_1 X_{t-1} + A_2 X_{t-2} + \ldots + A_p X_{t-p} + e_t$$
where e_t is a normally distributed multivariate white noise with covariance matrix Σ.

The large dimension (n=18 and p=4) of our VAR model implies that we face an issue of over-fitting due to the large number of parameters ('curse of dimensionality'). We address this issue by shrinking the model's coefficients toward those of the naïve and parsimonious random walk with drift model, $X_{it} = \delta_i + X_{i,t-1} + e_{it}$. De Mol et al. (2008) and Banbura et al. (2010) have shown that this approach reduces estimation uncertainty without introducing substantial bias.

The counterfactual (scenario)

The counterfactual is performed as follows. We simulate the model's parameters from their full posterior density, hence accounting for the estimation uncertainty of the hyperparameters. This approach is implemented using a simple Markov chain Monte Carlo algorithm. In particular, we use a Metropolis step to draw the low dimensional vector of hyperparameters (for details, see Giannone et al., 2010). Conditional on a value of the hyperparameters, the VAR coefficients can then be drawn from their posterior, which is normal-inverse-Wishart. Since we are interested in conditioning on the economic relationships prevailing before the last recession, the posterior is computed using the data until 2007:Q4.

For any given draw of the model's parameters from their posterior density, the draws from the counterfactual exercise are computed as conditional forecasts in which the conditioning information is given by the 1983:Q1-2007:Q4 history of all variables in the model and the observed outcomes of the level of real GDP and CPI until the end of the sample in 2013:Q3.

4.2 Eurozone: A policy problem

4.2.1 The Eurozone seen as a single economy

In this section, we first consider the Eurozone in aggregate and analyse the sectoral dynamics of savings and debt since the global recession of 2008 as well as the ECB policy in this context. Although we are aware that different countries within the monetary union entered the crisis with different levels of debt and followed different processes of adjustment, the aggregate perspective is of interest in itself given that monetary and financial regulatory policies operate at that level. Moreover, although fiscal and supply-side policies are decided at the national level and common policies have been influenced by distribution conflicts within the union, it is important to understand the ex post result of this complex policy process from the perspective of the union as a whole, since this understanding can help in evaluating the effectiveness of the tools of the monetary union in facing a debt crisis. In what follows, we will abstract from an analysis of political economy issues that may have constrained policy choices.

As described in Chapter 2, the ratio of total debt to GDP in the Eurozone increased rapidly in the pre-crisis years, driven by the build-up of private sector debt. However, the build-up of household debt was more muted than in the UK and the US, and the pre-crisis level lower.

Interestingly, unlike in the US, the ratio of total debt to GDP in the Eurozone is still higher today than before the crisis (Figure 4.7).

Figure 4.7   Eurozone total debt (% of GDP)

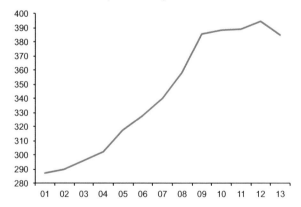

Source: Authors' calculation based on OECD, IMF and national accounts data. See Data Appendix at the end of the report.

In the first part of this section, we will analyse differences in balance sheet adjustment between the US and the Eurozone in order to shed some light on the different paths of debt adjustment in the two economies.

In the second part, we offer some considerations about future debt dynamics in the union and we conclude that, given current projections for inflation and potential output growth, the Eurozone finds itself in a situation of great fragility and with a lower debt-bearing capacity than the US.

Balance sheet adjustment since 2008: The Eurozone and the US

Let us recall the main facts regarding Eurozone debt dynamics post-crisis described by Figure 2.3: (i) household debt has stabilised in the Eurozone but, unlike in the US, it has not declined; (ii) public debt has increased in relation to GDP, although less than in the US; (iii) non-financial corporate debt has remained more or less flat; and (iv) financial-sector debt has started to adjust downwards only recently, but later and to a lesser extent than in the US.

These differences in post-crisis behaviour are the result of differences in pre-crisis balance sheet positions between the two economies and in sensitivity to asset price changes, together with differences in the fiscal, monetary and financial policy responses.

Households, housing prices and fiscal policy. Figure 4.8 shows that, pre-crisis, the household sector had built up a higher level of leverage in the US than in Eurozone, while the asset-to-income ratio was quite similar. The collapse of US household assets starts before the 2008 recession and corresponds to the decline in housing prices. Similarly, the recovery in household assets coincides with that of housing prices in 2012. In the Eurozone, household assets are more stable and less correlated with housing prices (which in any case, have shallower fluctuations than in the US). On the liabilities side, we see a downward adjustment in the US and a slow increase in the Eurozone which, having entered the crisis with a lower liability-to-income ratio, has now reached a similar ratio to the US.

Figure 4.9 shows that the household savings ratio increased from 2006 to 2012, corresponding to the phase of balance sheet adjustment. The deleveraging process is likely to have been facilitated by very aggressive fiscal policy. Indeed, Figure 4.9 also shows that, immediately after the crisis, the US fiscal deficit was almost double that of the Eurozone and the increase in savings in the household sector was almost matched by a decrease in the public sector. In contrast with the US, Eurozone households in 2009-10 decreased their saving rate and, as we have seen in Figure 4.8, increased their liabilities. Neither flow nor stock dynamics in the Eurozone correspond to the typical balance sheet adjustment, but rather to adjustment to protracted weak demand.

Figure 4.8   Household assets, liabilities and housing prices

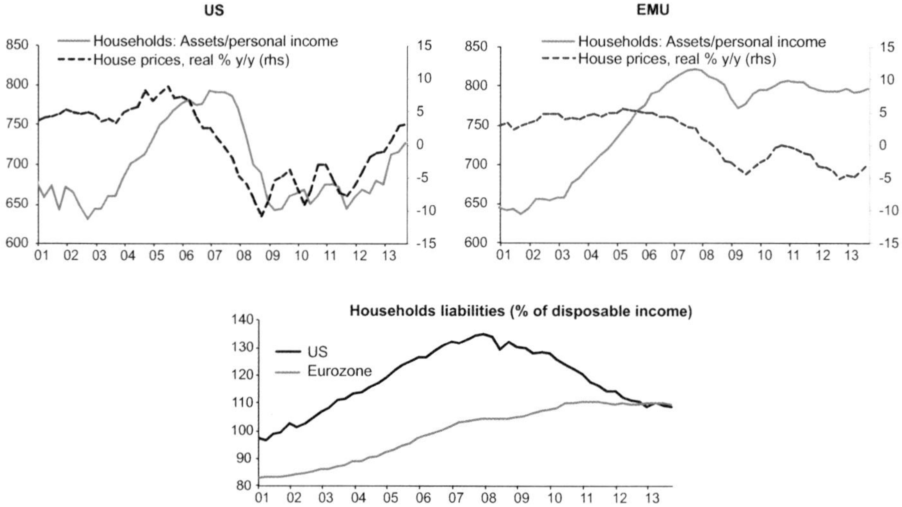

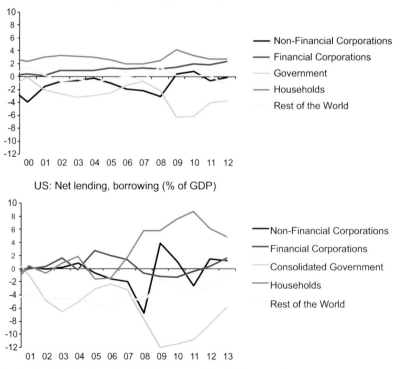

Source: Authors' calculations based on ECB, Eurostat and Federal Reserve data.

Figure 4.9   Eurozone financial flows

Source: Authors' calculations based on ECB, Eurostat and Federal Reserve data.

The US economy started a recovery by the third quarter of 2009 (according to the NBER), the fiscal deficit started shrinking by 2010 and US household assets started rebounding by the second half of 2011, while liabilities kept falling until 2013. In the Eurozone, the recovery started at the same time (according to CEPR), but household assets remained stable while liabilities kept increasing, private saving decreasing and public saving increasing (all relative to GDP). In the third quarter of 2011, the Eurozone entered a second recession. These facts suggest that, although Eurozone households entered the crisis in a more solid balance sheet position, their net worth deteriorated as a consequence of the protracted weakness of the real economy and conservative fiscal policy. If another global recession were to hit in the next few years, it will find Eurozone households in a more vulnerable situation than in 2008.

Non-financial corporations. In Chapter 2, we showed that non-financial corporations in the Eurozone built up liabilities before the crisis and, since then, have adjusted very little. From Figure 4.9, however, we can detect an adjustment in their savings behaviour. Indeed, non-financial corporations moved from a pre-crisis position of persistent negative savings to one of positive or zero savings. This adjustment is likely to reflect a situation of prolonged uncertainty that led to a decline in the investment rate (from 22.7% in 2007 to 19.2% in 2013). This contrasts with the US, where the savings behaviour of the corporate sector has been less persistent.

The financial sector and the role of the ECB. Figure 4.10 shows the asset-to-GDP ratios of financial corporations by category, where banks are labelled as 'Other MFI'.[20] Notice that the decline in the banks' asset-to-GDP ratio that started in 2012 was partly offset by the increase for other financial intermediaries (OFI).[21] The total size of the balance sheet of Eurozone financial intermediaries is still not much different from before the crisis.

---

20 MFIs are monetary financial intermediaries and include the European Central Bank, national central banks, credit institutions and money market funds.
21   OFI are intermediaries other than banks, pension funds, insurance or money market funds. They include corporations engaged in financial leasing, financial vehicles which are holders of securitised assets, financial holding corporations, dealers in securities and derivatives (when dealing for their own account), venture capital corporations and development capital companies.

Figure 4.10 Eurozone financial corporations: Assets by type of institution

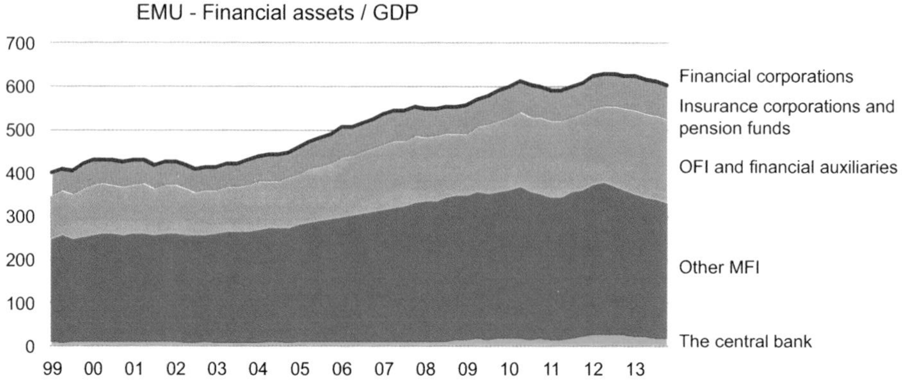

Source: Authors' calculations based on ECB and OECD data.

If we now look at the leverage of banks as measured by the capital-to-asset ratio and compare the Eurozone with the US (Figure 4.11), we can see a difference in both the timing and the size of the adjustment. Since comparing these ratios for the two economies is made difficult by differences in accounting standards, we report an index that sets both ratios at 100 in 2008. The chart shows that, while the US banking sector was recapitalised shortly after the Lehman event, the Eurozone banks have started this process only recently. The process of bank recapitalisation in the Eurozone is ongoing in the context of the Asset Quality Review and the stress tests that will be completed in October 2014. Some further deleveraging should therefore be expected in the near future.

There are of course reasons for the delayed action on the recapitalisation of banks in the Eurozone: the large size of individual banks relative to governments was a significant factor that made recapitalisation via public money difficult, but governance and structural factors (e.g. cross-shareholding arrangements typical in many Eurozone countries) were also obstacles to the initiation of a decisive process (Reichlin, 2014). Had a Eurozone mechanism for the resolution of banking crises been in place at that time, we would probably have seen more timely action and a more rapid adjustment of the financial sector. The discussion of the limits of the Eurozone institutional architecture and the role that these limits played during the crisis goes beyond the scope of this report. As food for thought for that discussion, however, it is interesting to observe that lack of aggressive action towards the banks did not spare the Eurozone from persistent declines in lending, although it is difficult to distinguish between the causes of weak lending to the real economy: limited supply of credit caused by under-capitalisation of the banking sector; increasing risks of credit related to the protracted weakness of the real economy; or lack of demand, also as a result of weakness in the real economy.

Figure 4.11 US and Eurozone bank capital-to-assets ratio

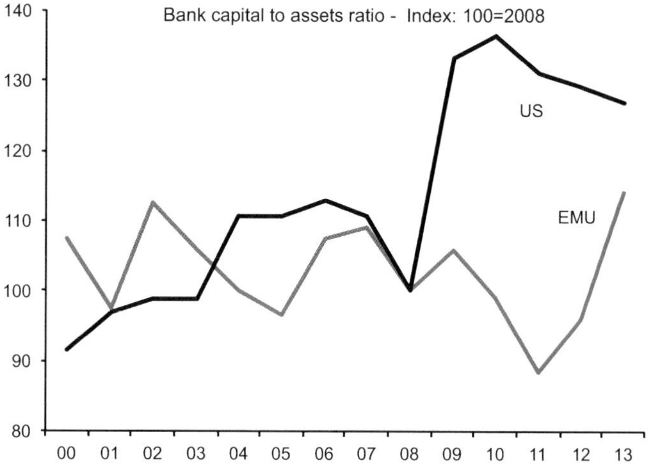

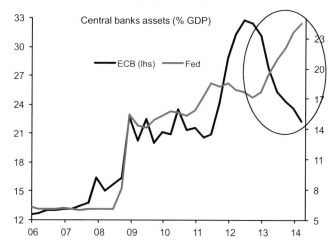

Source: Authors' calculations based on ECB and Federal Reserve data.

With fiscal policy action limited by the rules established by the Treaty and delayed action on bank recapitalisation, the ECB, as the only truly federal institution, had a large gap to fill. It is therefore interesting to consider the role of monetary policy in the adjustment of the financial sector. Figure 4.12 depicts the ratio of central bank assets to GDP for the Eurozone and the US.

Figure 4.12 ECB and Federal Reserve balance sheets

Source: Authors' calculations based on ECB, Federal Reserve and national accounts data.

The main 'non-standard' monetary policy tool used by the ECB since 2009 has been the long-term refinancing operations (LTROs). These are repo loans to banks, providing unlimited liquidity at a fixed rate for a given period of time and which leave the amount of liquidity in circulation entirely determined by banks' demand. The first LTRO, with a one-year term, was implemented in early 2009, a second wave was implemented in late 2011 to early 2012, with a three-year term. As a result, the balance sheet of the Eurosystem expanded meaningfully. Indeed, the expansion in that period is comparable with that of the Federal Reserve system resulting from quantitative easing. But, given the temporary nature of the LTROs and the option for banks to repay funds borrowed under the scheme, the ECB balance sheet started to shrink in 2012 in line with an easing of liquidity tensions and some banks repaying their loans. This removed excess liquidity in the system and put upward pressure on money market rates, effectively creating a monetary contraction.

Although aggressive ECB action was essential to save the financial system from collapse, there are two critical problems. First, there is evidence that the first wave of LTROs, implemented in the midst of the liquidity crisis following the Lehman collapse, was successful in relation to both financial stability and monetary policy.[22] As the crisis deepened, however, it became clear that solvency problems of sovereigns and banks were at the core of the financial crisis. Given the lack of government action and the constraints on other forms of ECB intervention, the LTROs were likely instrumental in preventing a collapse of the banking system, but they were neither adequate to deal with the solvency problems of banks, nor sufficient to avoid a fully fledged credit crunch.

Indeed, it can be argued that, in the absence of action to recapitalise the banks, one of the consequences of the LTROs was to keep insolvent banks alive, particularly in the euro periphery, and to delay the deleveraging of the banking sector. As shown above, financial debt remained almost constant in 2011-12.

The LTROs did not prevent a credit crunch in the economy, as the funds they provided were used to buy government bonds rather than to lend to the economy, as shown by the increase of the ratio of sovereign bonds to assets in the Eurozone banks' balance sheets (Figure 4.13). This change in asset composition, particularly strong in Spain and Italy, has been a significant feature of the Eurozone banks' adjustment and has involved, in particular, domestic sovereign bonds (see, amongst others, Battistini et al., 2014). As a consequence, as argued by Reichlin (2014), lending in the second recession was weaker than in the first if we control for the fact that the decline in real economic activity had been less pronounced (see Figure 4.14).

In sum, weak lending and a change in asset composition in favour of sovereign bonds are the result of a combination of factors: undercapitalisation in the banking sector; restrictive fiscal policy; geographical segmentation of financial markets leading to a high correlation between bank risk and sovereign risk; the ineffectiveness of monetary policy in this context; and persistent stagnation of the real economy. Progress has been made towards the establishment of the banking union which, together with the new European Systemic Risk Board, promises to lead to more timely action on banks in the future (although with much uncertainty related to the limited resources to be available for use in crisis resolution).

---

22 In a quantitative study, Giannone et al. (2012) have shown that the macroeconomic effect of these
    policies was small but significant.

Figure 4.13 Breakdown of Eurozone banks' assets

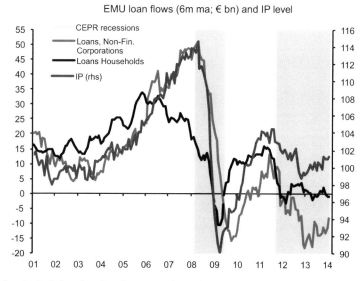

Source: Authors' calculations based on ECB data.

Figure 4.14 Eurozone loans and industrial production

Source: Authors' calculations based on Eurostat and ECB data.

Let us now come to the second problem. A new phase started in the second part of 2012. Given the temporary nature of the ECB LTRO programme and the option for banks to repay funds borrowed under that scheme, the Eurosystem balance sheet started to shrink. The contraction in the size of the Eurosystem balance sheet is striking if we compare it with the still ongoing expansion of the Federal

Reserve balance sheet (Figure 4.12). Although the Eurosystem entered the crisis with a larger balance sheet, its asset-to-GDP ratio is now around 20%, compared with a ratio of about 30% in the US. This contraction is a sign of stabilisation of the financial system and suggests that the liquidity crisis is over. This, combined with the recent recapitalisation process of the banking sector (still ongoing), suggests that the banking crisis is finally under control. However, the Eurozone still faces a more standard macroeconomic problem of protracted weakness of the real economy and very low inflation, below market and ECB expectations. In this context, a contraction of the balance sheet of the eurosystem that induces an upward pressure on market interest rates is not desirable. The ECB has recently announced a new set of non-standard measures, but the combination of high debt, low real growth and low inflation is still a reason for concern and calls for further action.

The future

The combination of structural factors, high initial leverage (corporates and banks especially) and the flaws of the Eurozone architecture which precluded a more aggressive policy response have meant that the crisis in the Eurozone has been more severe than elsewhere in the world; a 'Type 3' crisis (see Appendix 3A) with a much pronounced contraction of output and a more pronounced slowdown of potential output than in the US (Figure 4.15). From a bird's eye view, the output loss relative to previous trends is about 5 percentage points in the US and more than twice that in the Eurozone.

Figure 4.15   US and Eurozone output level

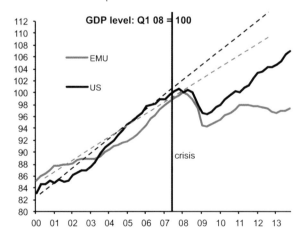

Source: Authors' calculations based on national accounts data.

Moreover, the severe demand contraction and consequent overcapacity has led to a situation of very low inflation. The result is a substantial slowdown of nominal growth to below 2%, which interacts perversely with the deleveraging process, being at the same time a hindrance to it and a consequence of it. As discussed in Chapter 3, a low nominal interest rate is little consolation when inflation is low and potential output growth declining. As for potential growth, beyond the effect of the last crisis, there are longer-term structural weaknesses that affect its future dynamics. Beside productivity developments, a key factor in this calculation is demographic developments, as indicated by World Bank projections (see Figure 4.16).

Figure 4.16 Eurozone demographics

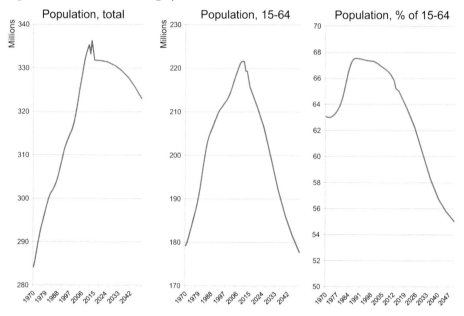

Source: World Bank.

Lower potential output growth has decreased the Eurozone debt-bearing capacity. By putting an upward pressure on real interest rates, declining inflation expectations will have a similar effect. Since projected output growth is lower than in the US and inflation expectations are weaker, debt-bearing capacity in the Eurozone is poised to be lower than in the US. This calls for difficult policy choices, which we discuss in Chapter 5.

The euro periphery. The worst legacy

If the aggregate Eurozone is a source of concern on account of the still high leverage ratios, the limited progress in deleveraging the financial sector, the negative impact of the associated credit crunch and the severe impact of the crisis on the real economy, all these problems look worse again in relation to the euro periphery. Indeed, the legacy of the two recent crises already experienced since 2008 means a chronic liability and economic slack overhang that will hamper macro-financial performance in the coming years. It also means vulnerability to any future spike in international funding conditions, given the major rollover exposures faced by these countries. The output losses since 2008 show completely different dynamics between the core and the periphery (Figure 4.17). Indeed, as shown in the chart, while German output is by now well above 2008:Q1 levels, and in France it has recovered the loss, in Greece it is about 25% below, in Italy about 9% below, and it is still well below in the other peripheral countries.

Figure 4.17   Eurozone and selected member countries' output levels

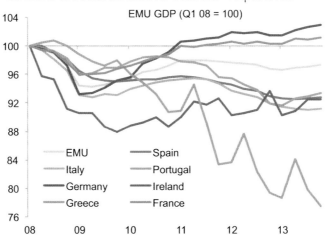

Source: Authors' calculations based on national accounts data.

As shown in Figure 4.18, the divergent core and periphery dynamics reflect, amongst other factors, a much more severe credit crunch, especially after 2011 (see the previous section). Figure 4.19 and Table 4.3 show the leverage dynamics and the sectoral composition of debt for selected European economies.

Figure 4.18 Bank lending in the Eurozone

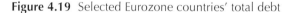

Bank Lending to the Private Sector (Q1 08 = 100)

Spain
Germany
France
Italy
Portugal
Ireland

Source: Authors' calculations based on ECB data.

Figure 4.19 Selected Eurozone countries' total debt

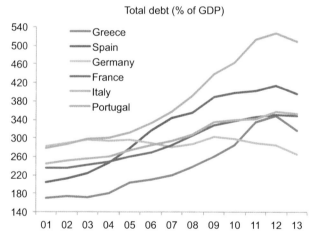

Total debt (% of GDP)

Greece
Spain
Germany
France
Italy
Portugal

Source: authors' calculations based on national accounts data. Ireland is excluded as an outlier

While Figure 4.20 shows that the debt levels of households and non-financial corporations in the euro periphery are a source of concern (especially in Ireland, Spain and Portugal), these countries are especially vulnerable due to their net international investment positions and levels of public debt, which are clearly more worrisome than anywhere else and increase vulnerability to future financial shocks (Figures 4.21 and 4.22).[23]

---

23 Ireland is not included in Figure 4.20 due to the outsized role of foreign multinational firms in the non-financial corporate sector. However, other evidence indicates that Irish households and many Irish small and medium-sized enterprises are highly indebted.

Table 4.3 Eurozone total debt breakdown

2013	Total a $= b+c$ $= d+e$	Domestic b	External c	Net external position	Financial d	Total ex-fin. $e = f+g$	Public f	Private $g = h+i$	Households h	Non-fin. companies i
Eurozone	**385**	**259**	**126**	**-19**	**128**	**257**	**93**	**164**	**64**	**100**
Ireland	1026	10	1016	-116	584	442	124	318	102	216
Netherlands	636	332	304	43	342	294	74	221	126	95
Portugal	507	276	232	-129	128	379	129	250	87	163
Belgium	408	162	246	45	58	350	102	248	56	192
Spain	394	229	166	-95	95	300	94	206	77	129
Italy	352	226	127	-34	94	258	133	125	45	81
France	347	146	202	-27	93	254	94	161	57	104
Greece	317	79	238	-121	13	304	175	129	64	65
Austria	315	119	197	-4	80	235	75	161	53	107
Finland	307	87	220	16	65	242	57	185	66	119
Germany	265	115	150	37	72	193	78	114	57	57

Source: Authors' calculations based on OECD, IMF and national accounts data.

Figure 4.20 Selected Eurozone countries' private debt

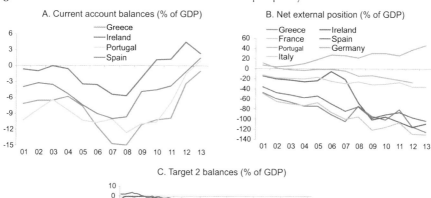

Source: Authors' calculations based on national accounts data.

Figure 4.21 External imbalances of the Eurozone periphery

Source: Authors' calculations based on IMF data and Eurocrisis Monitor Database.

Let us start by examining the dynamics of external liabilities. The boom-bust experience of the smaller euro periphery economies provides special insights into the dynamics of leverage for small open economies operating inside a currency union. While a currency union shares many characteristics of a fixed exchange rate regime, it is qualitatively different due to the existence of a common central bank that can provide cross-border liquidity flows in the event of a crisis.

Over 2003-07, Greece, Ireland, Portugal and Spain each experienced substantial net financial inflows, with an associated expansion in the scale of current account deficits and deterioration in their net international investment positions (see Figure 4.21).[24] These international flows were predominantly debt-type flows, with equity-type flows much smaller in scale (Lane, 2013).

Since 2008, there has been a sharp contraction in net capital flows, with these countries running current account surpluses by 2013. Significantly, the reversal in private capital flows was much larger than the overall reversal, since private outflows were partly substituted by official inflows. These official flows took two forms: ECB liquidity flows to banks in these countries (as shown in Figure 4.21), and EU-IMF loans to the national governments.

However, the legacy of the sustained period of current account deficits (in combination with the impact of stock-flow adjustments) is that the net international investment positions of these countries hover at around 100% of GDP. In turn, these accumulated net external liabilities represent a serious potential drag on future macroeconomic performance and financial stability.

Figure 4.22 Eurozone countries' public debt

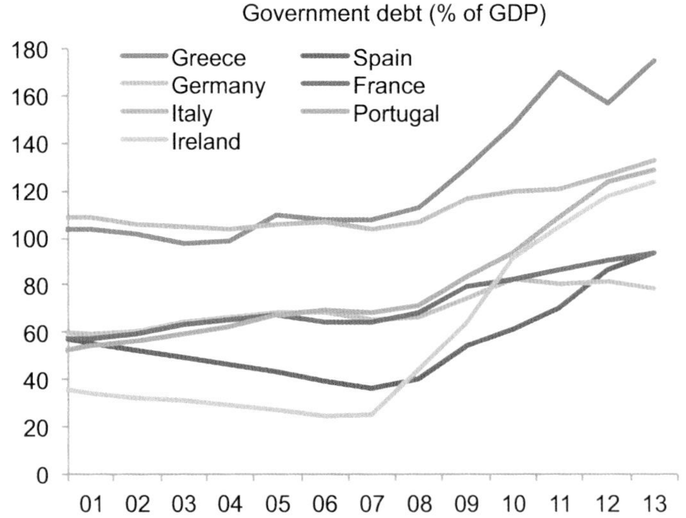

Government debt (% of GDP)

Source: Authors' calculations based on national accounts data.

It is important to appreciate that these aggregate external imbalances reflect a diversity of sectoral imbalances in the individual countries. However, a common pattern across the euro periphery has been that the crisis has resulted in a sharp rise in public debt (Figure 4.22). Indeed, not only is the ratio between public debt and GDP almost at or above 100% (with Greece and Italy the worst cases), but it

---

24   There was an earlier wave of capital inflows in the late 1990s associated with the convergence in interest rates triggered by the formation of the single currency (Blanchard and Giavazzi, 2001). However, the 2003-07 inflows were much larger in magnitude, despite a less attractive set of macroeconomic fundamentals relative to the earlier wave (Lane and Pels, 2012).

is also still rising. (While Italy is not similar to the euro periphery in relation to net international investment position, these countries are grouped together in relation to common concerns about public debt.)

In particular, Italy (133%), Portugal (129%) and Ireland (124%) look worrisome in terms of the level of public debt (considering also the very disappointing nominal growth trends), while the still high deficit in Spain means that its public debt trajectory remains a concern. Importantly, the efforts to deleverage the public sectors in these countries through government programmes have largely underachieved – the 2013 public debt ratios in Spain, Italy, Portugal and Greece exceeded the targets set early in 2012 by more than 10 percentage points. These debt dynamics reflect large overshooting in the fiscal deficit, particularly in Spain where the 2013 ratio was still twice as large as the target set only a year earlier (-7.0% versus a target of -3.0%). This overshooting reflects the adverse loop (see Section 5.1) between procyclical austerity measures and growth in the absence of other supportive policies. The large gaps between projections and outcomes provide a cautionary tale about the difficulty of reducing debt-to-income ratios sharply through austerity policies under such conditions.

Figures 4.23A and 4.23B show the evolution of debt levels over 2003-12 for the household sector and the non-financial corporate sector. Figure 4.23A shows that, in each country, household debt grew more rapidly than GDP during the 2003-07 pre-crisis period, with the expansion especially strong in Ireland (the debts were primarily accumulated to fund housing investment). Since the onset of the crisis, we can see some deleveraging in countries that have been more exposed to the housing crisis (Ireland, Spain and Portugal), while France and Italy have not adjusted and Greek leverage has been growing, driven by the collapse in the denominator rather than by extra consumer borrowing.

Figure 4.23 Eurozone countries' household and corporate debt

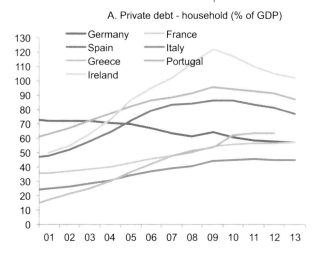

A. Private debt - household (% of GDP)

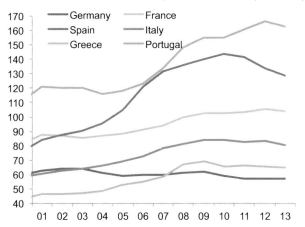

B. Private debt - corporate ex-financials (% of GDP)

Source: Authors' calculations based on national accounts data.

Figure 4.23 shows that non-financial corporates also accrued extra debt during 2003-07, but with the exception of France, this has stabilised since the crisis.[25]

Taken together, Section 4.2.2 has shown that the legacy of the crisis for the euro periphery is very high levels of sectoral debt and net external debt. Consistent with the overall themes of this report, these debt overhangs represent a substantial drag on the potential growth performance of this group. In addition, it renders the group vulnerable to the normalisation of global long-term interest rates and exposed in the event of a future disruption in international financial markets.

---

25 The sharp increase in the debt of non-financial corporates in Ireland since 2007 can be explained by the tax-driven financial engineering activities of the domestic affiliates of global firms, and is not matched by local firms.

4.3   Emerging markets: The next crisis?

Emerging economies were resilient to the 2008 financial crisis, but rising leverage is a concern

Compared to developed economies, the group of emerging economies was less vulnerable to the global financial crisis that took hold in 2007-08. This was no accident – in the wake of the 1990s emerging market crises, these countries took steps to limit debt levels. At the external level, aggregate net financial flows to emerging economies contracted (and turned into net outflows for a substantial number of countries), while the composition of external liabilities also shifted away from debt-type liabilities to equity-type liabilities (Lane and Milesi-Ferretti, 2007; Lane, 2013).

In addition, these countries also accumulated large stocks of foreign currency reserves, providing liquidity against the risk of a funding shock in foreign currency markets. The result was that many of these countries accumulated long net foreign currency positions, with foreign currency assets in excess of foreign currency liabilities, which was radically different to the 1990s situation (Lane and Shambaugh, 2010). The counterpart to this more cautious approach to taking on external debt was also a much more modest expansion in domestic credit during the pre-crisis period.

The lower vulnerability of emerging economies to the global financial crisis (and their faster subsequent recovery) provides an important lesson in terms of the advantages of maintaining a prudential approach to debt levels. However, developments since 2008 have led to concerns about increasing leverage in some of these countries. Along one dimension, a number of emerging economies reacted to the global crisis and the consequent slowdown in exports by switching from export-led growth to domestically led growth, engineered by a strong expansion in domestic credit, most noticeably in China. Along another dimension, the super-low interest rate environment in advanced economies has encouraged a new wave of debt issuance by firms in emerging economies. In contrast to the mid-2000s phase, this new wave of global liquidity has been primarily intermediated through the bond market rather than the international banking system (Shin, 2013).

The result was the strong increase in the ratio of total debt (ex-financials) to GDP for emerging economies, by a staggering 36% since 2008. Higher leverage, although helping to shield these economies from the chilling wind blowing from advanced economies, is an increasing concern in terms of the future risk profile given the ongoing steep slowdown of nominal growth, which reduces the 'debt capacity' of emerging economies exactly when they would need to expand it (see Chapter 3).

Moreover, a substantial proportion takes the form of offshore issuance through the foreign affiliates of domestic corporations (Bruno and Shin, 2014). These offshore liabilities pose an indirect risk to domestic financial stability in emerging markets, since a disruption in offshore funding would compromise the consolidated financial health of the issuing corporates, damaging economic performance and generating a reduction in corporate deposits in the domestic banking system (Shin, 2013). In terms of funding risks, the surge in issuance leaves these firms vulnerable to shifts in appetite among global bond investors, with the major international asset management firms the primary intermediaries in this market.

In what follows, we examine the most critical cases among the emerging economies: China and the so-called 'fragile eight' (Argentina, Brazil, Chile, India, Indonesia, Russia, South Africa and Turkey).

China: Between a rock (rising and high debt) and a hard place (lower growth)

China is emblematic of the leverage cycle that we depicted in Chapter 3 – its position in this cycle makes it one of the candidates for the next episode of the debt crises that have plagued the world since the early 1990s. As per our taxonomy in Appendix 3A, a debt crisis does not necessarily involve massive defaults and/or contractions of output. In the case of China, if such a crisis were to occur in the relatively near term, it could plausibly take the form of a 'Type 2' crisis (as in Japan; see Appendix 3A), although not necessarily to the same extent and only if policymakers insist in leveraging up the economy for a prolonged period of time with the aim of keeping growth artificially high. Such adjustment would possibly be made easier by an increase in inflation and a depreciation of the exchange rate. However, a significant slowdown of Chinese activity and a depreciation of the currency would have a large impact on the world economy.

Let us go through all the steps of the analysis leading to these conclusions. Thanks to the positive supply-side shocks stemming from the opening to free markets at the end of the 1980s compounded at the end of 2001 by the accession to the WTO, China boosted its real growth rate well into double digits until 2007. The top panel of Figure 4.24 shows an acceleration of real GDP growth over that period, as measured by different filtering techniques. The bottom panel of the same figure shows that nominal growth accelerated as well.

Figure 4.24 Measures of real and nominal GDP growth in China

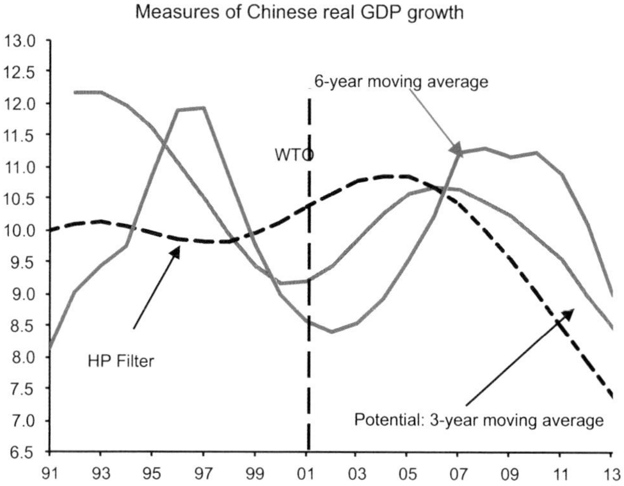

Measures of Chinese real GDP growth

6-year moving average

WTO

HP Filter

Potential: 3-year moving average

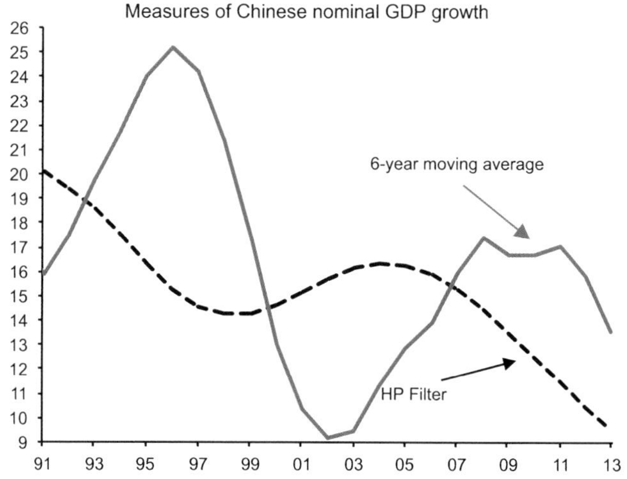

Measures of Chinese nominal GDP growth

6-year moving average

HP Filter

Source: Authors' calculations based on OECD and national accounts data.

The acceleration of potential growth is consistent with strong data on productivity and demographic growth in the first half of the first decade of this century (see Figure 4.25). In this period of strong, organic expansion, leverage in the Chinese economy was consistently stable.

Consistent with the 'leverage cycle' hypothesis (see Chapter 3), it was only when growth started to fade that China decided to 'fight the trend' by leveraging up. In particular, the 2008 debt crisis in advanced economies hurt Chinese exports at a time when the productivity boost stemming from the WTO accession and the impulse from demographics were about to turn.

Figure 4.25 Productivity growth and the share of working age population

China: Productivity growth (%y/y)

%   Share of working age population: 5-year changes

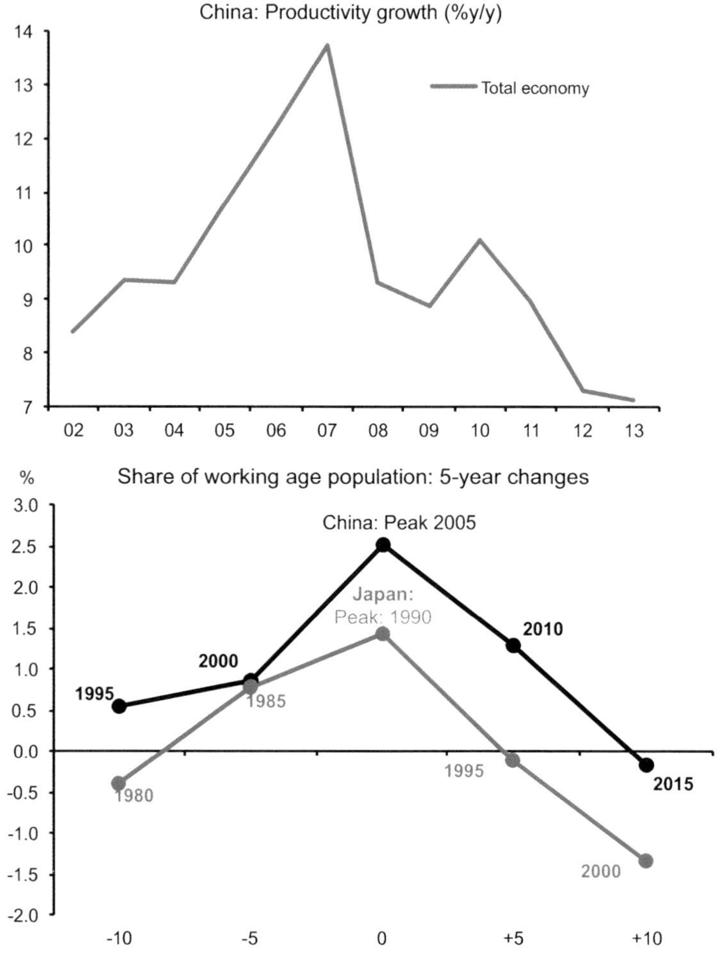

Source: Authors' calculations based on national accounts and World Bank data.

Since 2008, Chinese total debt (ex-financials) has increased by a stunning 72% of GDP (Figure 4.26), or 14% per year, a shift almost double that experienced by the US and UK in the six years that preceded the beginning of their financial crisis in 2008.

This brisk acceleration has brought the overall leverage of the Chinese economy to almost 220% of GDP, almost double the average of other emerging markets (see Figure 2.23 and Table 2.1)

The stunning increase in leverage since 2008 arguably came at the cost of an inefficient use of resources, as is often the case when leverage increases at a quick pace. Moreover, the increase coincided with the shift from export-orientated growth to domestically orientated growth. This possibly exacerbated the overinvestment problem in China and created conditions of overcapacity in a number of sectors.

Figure 4.26 Chinese total debt and breakdown

China: Total debt ex-financials (% iof GDP)

220
210
200
190
180
170
160
150
140

+72%

05   06   07   08   09   10   11   12   13

China: Total debt ex-financials breakdown (% of GDP)

180
160
140
120
100
80
60
40
20

Private

Public (central and local governments)

02   03   04   05   06   07   08   09   10   11   12   13

Source: Authors' calculations based on national account data.

Indeed, while investment in previous years was mostly concentrated in manufacturing and in sectors affected by the additional demand created by the export boom following the WTO accession, the credit boom in 2008 and thereafter spurred huge investments in housing and infrastructure. These sectors, although effective in supporting the economy in the short term, failed to boost potential output and actually created excess capacity in related sectors, like steel. In turn, overcapacity in a number of key sectors led to downward pressure on production prices. Since 2008, the slowdown in measures of growth to about 7% (Figure 4.24) has been accompanied by a fall in underlying domestic price pressures and slower growth in nominal GDP.

As a consequence, China is facing a poisonous combination of high, fast-growing leverage and slowing nominal GDP (Figure 4.27). This, in turn, suggests growing difficulties in servicing and repaying debt in a number of sectors in the future are likely. These difficulties might be exacerbated by the fact that market rates are likely to increase as a consequence of ongoing financial reforms.

Figure 4.27 Chinese leverage and underlying nominal GDP growth

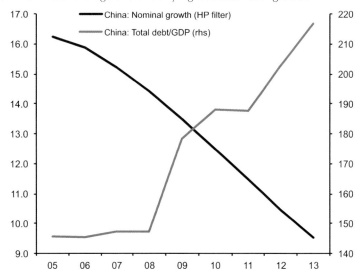

Source: Authors' calculations based on national account data.

In addition to these patterns, the debt situation in China is made even more fragile by two further considerations. First, the recent increase in debt was raised especially by relatively weak borrowers, such as local governments with fragile income streams and, in particular, companies active in construction and other sectors (e.g. the steel producing industry) plagued by overcapacity (the driver of private debt in Figure 4.26). Second, credit was granted by relatively weak lenders, as shown by the sharp increase of the weight of shadow banking (trust funds, etc.) within total lending (Figure 4.28).

These factors help to explain the Chinese effort for structural reforms aiming at supporting potential growth and breaking the formation of a vicious spiral between leverage and growth. The success of this effort will be crucial to the future of China. However, it is legitimate to be sceptical about the potential of reforms to boost short-term growth, even reforms that are successful in the medium term.

In China, as elsewhere, it is hard to identify in advance the leverage breaking point beyond which a crisis enfolds. It is less hard, however, to interpret the current debt dynamics of debt as unsustainable. Most likely, the Chinese government is aware of the adverse dynamics that we have described and is willing to start a process of deleveraging. At least initially, this process should be in the form of a moderation in the pace of the leveraging up of the economy. However, there will be a price to pay for this policy since slower credit formation, the main support for growth in recent years, would likely translate into a substantial slowdown in activity.

Figure 4.28 Chinese debt breakdown by lenders

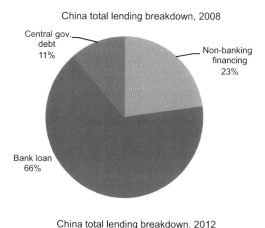

China total lending breakdown, 2008

Central gov.
debt
11%

Non-banking
financing
23%

Bank loan
66%

China total lending breakdown, 2012

Central gov
debt
7%

Non-banking
financing
33%

Bank loan
60%

Source: Authors' calculations based on national data.

This takes us to the difficult analysis of what lies ahead for China, or better, what kind of crisis we should expect. Following our taxonomy in Appendix 3A, should we expect full-blown 'Type 1' or 'Type 3' crisis, or a slow-burn 'Type 2' crisis?

The breakdown of the Chinese debt displayed in Table 2.1 offers some crucial elements for the analysis. Let us highlight the following facts: (a) the government has a low debt relative to GDP (49% of GDP if one includes local governments, 26% for the central government only); and (b) Chinese debt is virtually all domestic, similar to that of Japan. These conditions mean that the central government has at the current stage the resources to contain systemic risk (for instance, intervening to avoid a 'too-big-to-fail' default) and that policymakers have very little incentive to proceed towards an explicit default, since it would hurt mainly domestic investors. Therefore, a Russian or an Argentine default scenario is not likely since in both those cases, the bulk of debt was held by foreign investors, which typically provides an incentive for explicit defaults. A more likely scenario for China is a combination of inflation and currency depreciation that indirectly shifts the burden of the adjustment to foreigners.

In order to contain systemic risk, the Chinese government may choose to bail out some major players (either financial or non-financial) if high debt and slowing nominal growth result in some over-leveraged large entities getting in trouble. However, even if such bailouts stemmed from systemic risk, it would not be a free ride. Indeed, a combination of public bailouts and the likely burning of private shareholders would correspond to a diminished propensity to lend in the private sector and an increased perception of risk that would compound the slowdown in activity. The consequent deleveraging would be accentuated should there be, as looks likely, a sequence of relatively 'small' defaults by individual private entities, which the government calculates would not threaten financial stability. Although not systemic, these defaults could still affect confidence and thus activity levels.

If rapid leveraging up was indeed the reason why China kept growing at a slowing, but above potential, rate since 2008, a phase of deleveraging through slower credit formation would imply a significant slowdown, with growth possibly falling below potential. Even a Chinese 'Type 2' crisis that avoided severe financial disruption but generated a significant growth slowdown would still have a global impact. The difference with the post-2008 crisis would be in the transmission channel: while the financial spillovers were the main transmission channel to the rest of the world in the advanced-economy crisis, the international transmission of deleveraging in China would primarily operate through lower demand for global exports. Given the prominence of China as a source of export demand in recent years, this would have a material impact on global growth performance. Furthermore, the combination of a trade slowdown and a renminbi depreciation could also generate international political economy tensions by triggering renewed debate about 'currency wars'.

It is also possible to envisage more adverse scenarios in which the Chinese authorities decide to fight the ongoing structural slowdown by maintaining the pace of leveraging up of the economy of recent years. Such a choice would increase the likelihood of a postponed, but abrupt 'Type 3' crisis down the road, as after another few years of rapid leveraging up even China would be unlikely to have the resources to achieve a gradual deleveraging process. Chinese policymakers are likely to remain for some time between the 'rock' of slowing nominal growth and the 'hard place' of high and rising leverage.

The 'fragile eight'

Recent market concerns have focused on the so-called 'fragile eight' (Argentina, Brazil, Chile, India, Indonesia, Russia, South Africa and Turkey) for which various types of risk indicators have shown significant movement since 2010, even if the individual circumstances of these countries are quite diverse. Accordingly, we also examine the behaviour of two subgroups of emerging economies (EM1 and EM2), where EM1 consists of the 'fragile eight' and EM2 consists of a second group of emerging markets that have shown more stable trajectories over this period (though risk assessments vary quite widely within this group). The EM1 and EM2 groups are listed in the Data Appendix.

Figure 4.29 shows the current account balance and the net international investment position for the EM1 and EM2 groups. The former has moved into a current account deficit since 2010 and experienced a substantial decline in its net international investment position since 2008; the latter remains in a current account surplus and maintains a positive net international investment position.

Figure 4.29 Emerging market current account and net international investment positions

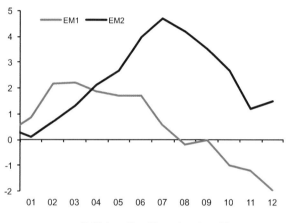

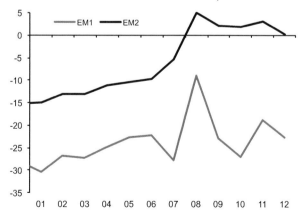

Source: Authors' calculations based on national accounts and IMF data.

The rise of emerging markets in international debt issuance since 2008 has been remarkable. Figure 4.30A shows the shares of the EM1 and EM2 groups in global cross-border bond portfolios, which have more than doubled since 2008. Figures 4.30B, 4.30C and 4.30D show the stocks of outstanding debt securities for the

EM1 and EM2 groups for the government sector, non-financial corporates and financial corporates. These charts underline that it is the private sector that is behind the surge in debt issuance in these countries in recent years.

The scale of recent cross-border flows and debt issuance by these countries remains modest relative to the levels attained by advanced economies over the 2003-07 period, while the structural changes in the financial systems of these economies (a deeper pool of domestic institutional investors, a greater role for local-currency bonds) also provides some degree of insulation against external shocks (International Monetary Fund, 2014a).

At the same time, the less liquid nature of the financial systems in emerging economies, the heavier reliance on foreign-currency debt (relative to advanced economies) and the more limited tolerance for large-scale exchange rate fluctuations mean that this increase in leverage generates vulnerabilities for this group. The May 2013 'taper tantrum' illustrated the market movements that can be associated with surprise shifts in the pace of normalisation in the international financial system, while a major open question for these economies is whether the level of funding availability for emerging economies might contract as interest rates go up in the major advanced economies.

In this regard, it is important to understand the shift in the investor base for emerging market debt, with the transition from bank-intermediated lending to the bond market (Shin, 2013; International Monetary Fund, 2014). In particular, the behaviour of mutual funds, hedge funds and other types of asset managers (both long-only and leveraged) is a critical factor in determining the stability/ instability of capital flows to this group.

Figure 4.30   Emerging market stock in outstanding debt securities

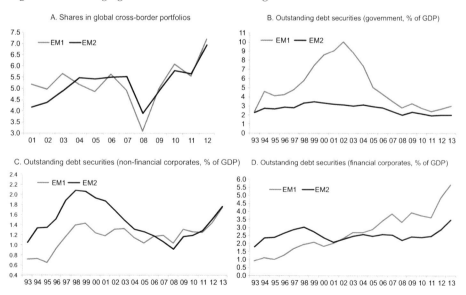

Source: Coordinated Portfolio Investment Survey (CPIS) and BIS securities database.

5 Policy issues

5.1 What have we learnt from past crises?

In our report we have focused on both the debt build-up preceding the last 'great' crisis and the post-crisis adjustment. Our analysis suggests that, pre-crisis, debt in advanced economies had increased above their capacity to bear it. Amongst emerging markets, China may now be in a similar situation and other countries in that group also show signs of fragility.

From an ex ante perspective, policymakers must seek to prevent excessive debt accumulation because this makes the economy vulnerable to macroeconomic and/or asset price shocks which, in turn, may require subsequent painful adjustment.[27] Ex post, if an adjustment must take place, policy also has a role to play in alleviating its costs to the economy. Our case studies evaluate the results of different policy choices and point to difficult trade-offs between further debt accumulation to prevent stagnation of the real economy and debt consolidation at the cost of stagnation.

In what follows, we highlight the main policy lessons that we draw from the experience of the last 20 years.

(i) Preventing excessive leverage and debt crises

In effect, it is a policy decision to let a country lever up above its means (that is, above its debt capacity). This may happen because policymakers view extremely high economic growth rates and advantageous borrowing conditions as permanent rather than temporary (as was the case in Ireland and Spain during the convergence period and after the launch of the euro), or because they use leverage to try to fight a persistent private-sector slowdown (as in China since 2008), or perhaps because they are just trying to squeeze the benefits of financial innovation to grow above the potential rates determined by the supply side of the economy, as was the case in the US at the beginning of this century. Moreover, in some cases, policymakers acted as cheerleaders for the process of excesses in the private sector and exposed the balance sheets of central and local governments to similar vulnerabilities. Thus, a clear-eyed recognition of the actual debt capacity

---

27 The political economy of debt management is made more complex by the possible interconnections between the growth in household debt and underlying shifts in income distribution (see, amongst others, Rajan, 2010).

of a country is the best preventive measure to guard against excessive leverage and the formation of a crisis.

However, it is impossible to understand trends in debt accumulation, particularly in the household sector, without appreciating the increase in size and leverage of the financial sector. Financial regulations aiming at increasing the resilience of the financial sector are a key ingredient in preventing excessive debt.

Given the difficulties in predicting the timing and incidence of crises, a primary policy goal is to ensure that macro-financial systems are resilient in the event of a crisis. Policy measures to improve resilience include efficient liquidity provision by monetary authorities, adequate capitalisation levels and orderly resolution schemes for distressed banks, bankruptcy laws that can efficiently address private-sector debt burdens and, in related fashion, a sovereign debt restructuring mechanism (see also Lane, 2013; CIEPR, 2013). At the international level, access to foreign currency liquidity can be provided by a network of currency-swap arrangements across central banks and lines of credit from a sufficiently well-funded IMF (see also Farhi et al., 2011).

The same motivation applies to fiscal discipline. A strong public sector balance sheet helps to make a country more resilient in the face of shocks. In the case of China, for instance, the low level of central government leverage is an element of strength amid the possibility of strains in other sectors of the economy, as it was in the cases of Spain and Ireland, which entered the crisis with low levels of public debt. Accordingly, ensuring that fiscal policy is run in a disciplined, counter-cyclical manner remains a high priority for policymakers and political systems.

The last crisis showed that banking regulations and fiscal discipline are not sufficient tools for crisis prevention and has led to a new focus on macroprudential regulation. However, while the principles of macroprudential regulation are straightforward, it is difficult to identify effective intervention mechanisms and to ensure that such interventions are skillfully implemented. For instance, a basic problem is the leakiness of macroprudential policies, with a tightening of regulations on banks driving activities away from banks towards various shadow banking activities or from domestic intermediaries to foreign intermediaries. In relation to the latter, it is important that foreign regulators follow the lead of the domestic regulator and ensure that foreign lending into an economy adheres to the principles laid out by the domestic regulator; in principle, this type of international coordination should be more effective under the Basel III set of international rules. At the European level, the new Single Supervisory Mechanism (SSM) should directly ensure that all Eurozone banks follow the same rule book, including any prescribed restrictions on geographical patterns in lending.

In relation to emerging markets, given the implementation difficulties facing macroprudential interventions, there has also been renewed interest in the potential for capital flow management tools as a device to limit excessive debt accumulation. However, capital controls also face their own types of implementation problems, so that it is not obvious that capital controls can be effectively deployed across a broad range of circumstances.

Another important tool for crisis prevention is credible debt restructuring mechanisms. The existence of such mechanisms is in itself a powerful deterrent to the accumulation of excessive debt, given that it makes investors and debtors more clearly exposed to the consequences of default, thereby mitigating moral hazard problems.

While robust debt restructuring mechanisms should reduce the frequency and scale of bailouts, it remains the case that limited and conditional bailouts may sometimes remain the least worst policy option during a crisis (Tirole, 2012). In particular, systemic risk factors and the fear of contagion can prompt a government to bail out individual banks or even non-bank debtors. Similarly, at the international level, sovereigns may receive official funding from the international system in order to avoid the disruptions associated with non-orderly defaults.

(ii) Managing deleveraging and debt crises

An important element in the dynamics of the leverage cycle is a slowness to recognise that income prospects deteriorated. If debt capacity is set back, either with a reduction that falls below the current level of debt or one constraining future debt accumulation (a lower target), then there is scope for policy to offset some of the adverse consequences for economic activity.

As shown in the schematic below, there are three stages in the process of coping with the leverage cycle. The first is the recognition that debt capacity has declined. The same calculation of the net present value of future output that matters for determining debt capacity also comes into play for calculating the market value of assets, such as equities and homes. As a consequence, simultaneously with the recognition that borrowing capacity has fallen, there will be a wealth loss as those capital values are written down. When those assets serve as collateral, there are additional hits to credit intermediation. The prospect for repayment diminishes with the declines in debt capacity and the value of the collateral securing those loans.

Figure 5.1 Stages of the leverage cycle

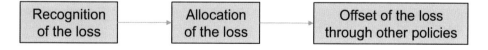

Policymakers can facilitate the recognition of these losses in their role as prudential supervisors. This is where stress tests of financial intermediaries enter as a means for the joint acknowledgement of asset impairment. In that regard, the initial asset and liability review in the US provides a model of the strict grading of a test with an option to fill the hole with government resources. In the event, because the aggregate deficiency was below the resources available through the Troubled Asset Recovery Program, the private sector provided the funding given the reassurance that failure was not an option. The asset quality review currently under way in Europe provides an opportunity to live up to that standard.

The issue of how to allocate the losses, which is the next stage in the process, is obviously complex. At the macroeconomic level, they have to be allocated so as to minimise a credit crunch. However, the pursuit of this objective may lead to controversial distributional consequences, such as penalising consumers/taxpayers to the benefit of private creditors. The experience of some of the countries in the Eurozone periphery is an example of this problem. Any losses in asset values and in the net present value of future income, or less-than-previously-anticipated gains, have to be apportioned among the various sectors of the economy. The three candidates are the original holders of those claims in the private sector, the government (or, more aptly, the ultimate obligor – the taxpayer), or the central bank through loans or asset market purchases. The problem of the allocation of losses is particularly complex in the Eurozone since creditors and debtors have a clear geographical identity and mostly share a common currency. Once losses are realised and allocated, there is scope for other policies to offset the macroeconomic consequences, the third stage in the process. The options here include fiscal expansion, which might be problematic given the increase in debt associated with the rescue of financial entities, or monetary policy accommodation.

The most straightforward way of thinking about the deleveraging policy problem is to consider the debt-to-income ratio, as in the next schematic. The essence of the recognition of a reduction in debt capacity is also the realisation that the ratio of debt-to-income cannot reach the level previously expected. A ratio can be adjusted either via the numerator or the denominator.

Figure 5.2   Debt and growth nexus

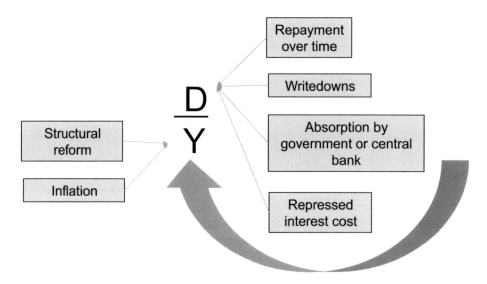

In terms of the numerator (the right side of Figure 5.2), four options are available. Debt can be paid down (if the problem is a lower level of debt capacity) or accumulated less rapidly (if the problem is a lower target debt capacity). Here, credit-income feedback dynamics intrude. If loans are expanding more slowly or being repaid on net, then headwinds created for aggregate demand that pulls GDP down relative to its prior trajectory. More directly, the value of debt could be written down in a credit event. But the debt of one entity is another's asset, and the direct reduction in asset values and any indirect spillover to other markets represents an immediate impediment to economic expansion. Moreover, the credit event may have a long shadow to the extent that market participants demand higher risk premiums in the future.

Either effort to trim back the path of debt tends to reduce nominal GDP relative to its prior path. As a consequence, it is not obvious that the ratio of debt to nominal GDP – the main metric of leverage adopted in this report – will decline. The most prominent case is fiscal austerity, which is the effort to reduce the public sector's portion of debt in the numerator. Fiscal consolidation tends to be associated with short-run income contraction so the impact on the debt-to-income ratio is problematic.

As shown repeatedly in this report, we observe a poisonous combination – globally and in almost any one geographic area – between high and higher debt/GDP and slow and slowing (both nominal and real) GDP growth, which stems from a two-way causality between leverage and GDP: on the one hand, slowing potential growth and falling inflation make it harder for policies to engineer a fall in the debt-to-GDP ratio, and on the other hand attempts to delever both the private sector (especially banks) and the public sector (through austerity measures) encounter headwinds, as they slow, if not compress, the denominator of the ratio (GDP). The euro periphery is where this perverse loop of debt and growth is most severe. It could also soon become acute in China.

An incorrect blend or sequence of anti-crisis policies (see below) would at the same time hurt the deleveraging effort and maximise output costs, worsening the 'type' of the crisis and thus the deviation from the pre-crisis output path (see Appendix 3.A in Chapter 3).

The economic equivalent of write-downs could be accomplished if the government absorbed the losses directly – e.g. the US taking the mortgage-related government sponsored enterprises under conservatorship – or indirectly through central bank acquisition – e.g. the Federal Reserve's purchase of mortgage-backed securities. The former represents a command on future tax revenue, in that the government debt has to be serviced. The latter represents a different kind of inter-temporal trade, since the central bank either has to pare back its balance sheet at some point in the future (presumably when the economy is better positioned to absorb the blow) or risk an increase in the price level in the long run. The lack of either form of support in the Eurozone, and especially of forms of quantitative easing – either bank loans or government bonds – has contributed to the development of a severe credit crunch and the establishment of a perverse loop with growth, at odds with the credit expansion which has resumed at a relatively early stage in the US (see Chapter 4).

A subtler outcome is the interest cost on government debt being reduced by encouraging the increase in the general price level even as it tilts incentives toward increased ownership of domestic currency nominal government debt through regulatory policy. The net result – financial repression – is often the recourse for governments burdened by debt (Reinhart and Sbrancia, 2014). The effect on the numerator of the ratio is to lower the path of debt over time by lowering the interest-service cost.

The difficulty of working on the numerator makes focusing on the denominator especially seductive. This is most likely why countries under pressure, and under IMF direction, promise structural reform in order to increase the real GDP component over time. The evidence for growing out of a debt problem, however, is limited. Reinhart et al. (2012) examined the experience of 22 industrial economies from 1800 to 2010: in only two cases of 26 sustained debt overhangs in their sample was the ratio of debt to income reduced by a pick-up in economic growth. If real activity cannot grow sufficiently, an alternative is to encourage its nominal value to scale up. Historically, inflation is often the recourse for governments burdened by high levels of debt and is the companion to financial repression.

In order to minimise the output losses of deleveraging policies, let alone of a crisis, a comparison of the recent experiences in the US and the Eurozone shows that a blend of policies has to be put in place: gradual deleveraging of the public sector (striking the right balance between long-term expenditure cuts and taxation measures so as to avoid an excessively procyclical impact on GDP), banking system restructuring (recapitalisation, bad banks and other measures), and monetary expansion (encompassing forms of outright monetary and credit easing) so as to minimise the adverse macro-financial impact of a credit crunch. All three strands of policy must be in place when both the public sector and the private sector need to be deleveraged. Still, eventually, overall deleveraging is required rather than a mere swap from private to public balance sheets.

Timing is of the essence, since early action and the correct sequencing of policy implementation matters for the minimisation of output costs. Ideally, it is advisable first to implement supportive banking and monetary policies, so that credit can flow again and provide renewed support to activity. Only then should fiscal policy gradually turn contractionary, since a recovering economy is better able to absorb the associated drag on growth. By and large, this was the policy mix put in place in the US (even if the timing of fiscal adjustment was arguably still too early relative to the ideal path), while fiscal austerity came before the restructuring of the banking system in the Eurozone, which adversely affected output dynamics.

Even with a supportive policy package, the deleveraging process can be painful and long-lasting. In the US, for instance, the deleveraging of the public sector balance sheet (both government and Federal Reserve), which was inflated in the past phase so as to give time to the private sector to start the process of deleveraging and prevent a credit crunch, has yet to occur and it is poised to be a long-lasting and risky process. In other terms, the 'exit' for both fiscal and monetary policy is just beginning.

Needless to say, this ideal sequencing is only feasible if the central government balance sheet is strong enough to be leveraged up initially and thus contribute to the deleveraging of the private sector. This was the case in Spain, for instance, where public debt was very low at the beginning of the crisis, which allowed the country to run larger deficits for longer, but not in Italy, which was forced into steeper austerity and thus recession. In China, as mentioned above, the low debt of the central government is a source of strength.

Sometimes, the ideal set of policies is prevented by the institutional setup. In the Eurozone, for instance, the sequencing was jeopardised by the reluctance of policymakers of core countries to put in place any form of transfer (either fiscal or monetary) to the periphery. Indeed, it can be argued that the fear that at some stage transfers would be necessary induced European policymakers to force a steeper-than-necessary public sector deleveraging in the periphery. By the same token, the possibly asymmetric impact of QE across member countries is a political barrier to the introduction of non-standard monetary measures by the ECB, a complicating factor not faced by the central banks of politically integrated economies (such as the US, the UK or Japan).

5.2   Policy options. Where are we now?

There is still a lot of work to do for policymakers. The legacy of the crisis is still a major issue for a number of developed economies – especially in the euro periphery – which remain extremely vulnerable, and ahead of the next financial crisis, with early signs already visible this time around in some emerging economies and especially in China.

Since the above-mentioned adverse combination of leverage and slower nominal GDP has hurt global debt capacity, the path for successful deleveraging policy looks quite narrow; indeed, there is a high likelihood of either a prolonged period of very low growth or even another global crisis.

Policymakers are deeply divided on how to address the combination of high debt, weak nominal growth and abundant global liquidity. The discussion is made difficult by the uncertainty about the strength of the recovery in developed markets and about the nature of the slowdown in some emerging markets.

We discuss below some key policy issues.

Issue 1. Monetary policy

Interest rates are at an historically low level and influential institutions (most notably, the Bank for International Settlements) have warned that the world is again in a situation in which a protracted low interest rate environment is creating incentives for investors in search of yield to take excessive risk. According to this view, financial regulation is not sufficient to prevent new excesses in leverage, while central banks in countries where the economy is strengthening, such as the US and the UK, should envisage an exit from very accommodative monetary policies.

In contrast with this view, the exceptional weakness of the recovery – as revealed, for example, by the persistence of low labour market participation rates in the US and underemployment in the UK – suggests that an accommodative monetary stance may be necessary for an extended period (International Monetary Fund 2014b). The weakness of the recovery calls for policies aiming at supporting aggregate demand and delaying exit (Summers, 2013; Krugman, 2014). In this report, we have argued that potential output growth in advanced economies has been on a declining trend for decades, accelerating after the crisis, with structural forces putting downward pressure on the natural rate of interest. In such a context, and with leverage still very high, allowing the real rate to rise above its natural level would risk killing the recovery, pushing the economy into a prolonged period of stagnation while putting at risk the already challenging deleveraging process. Although there is a lot of uncertainty over these quantities, our call is for caution. The case for caution in pre-emptively raising interest rates is reinforced by the weakness of inflationary pressures.

The policy question is whether monetary policy can remain accommodative while at the same time acting to prevent the rise of new bubbles via macroprudential tools. Since central banks have developed a new set of tools aimed at multiple targets, this should in principle be possible. However, we are in uncharted territory and vigilance is required in the monitoring of the observed growth in asset prices in various market segments and regions.

Beside this tension between monetary policy and financial stability objectives, whatever the interest rate path judged appropriate, it will be difficult for the Federal Reserve to delink market interest rate dynamics from the path of exit from quantitative easing and instability in financial markets. When the Fed raises rates, it will likely have a balance sheet of around $4.5 trillion, or a quarter the size of nominal GDP. It will accomplish policy firming by increasing the interest rates it pays on excess reserves and at its fixed-rate allotment facility. That is, the Fed will run a massive rolling book of reverse repo transactions and term deposits.

More generally, the reality is that the events of the past few years have redefined the term 'unusual'. The Fed will be expected to do more in the future than was expected under the settled notion of appropriate central banking before the crisis. Because it acted in extreme ways during the period of duress, it will be expected to step up at the next time of stress. With its balance sheet large and complicated, central bank officials might consider expanding the range of policy instruments. Federal Reserve officials will have to take account of the net consequences of the functioning of the market and the precedents they are setting.

The response to the last crisis illustrates that the dividing line between monetary and fiscal policy becomes very thin in exceptional circumstances.

To an important degree, the Federal Reserve's quantitative easing should be viewed as a second-best attempt to deal with collateral troubles associated with borrowers with debt greater than the value of their homes. Now that US home values at the national level have expanded at a double-digit pace but headwinds still seem evident, a more direct approach that is closer to the first-best solution of mortgage relief for still-stressed households might be in order.

Relative to the US, the policy mix in the Eurozone was much less effective in cushioning the impact of the financial crisis while at the same time putting economies on a sustainable path of deleveraging. Indeed, the double whammy of procyclical fiscal austerity and a credit crunch has made the deleveraging process much more costly. In turn, this has exacerbated the slowdown in nominal GDP, by both undermining the potential rate of growth and favouring excessive disinflationary pressures. Although a number of institutional constraints in the design and functioning of the monetary union have contributed to this unfortunate policy mix, it is important for the Eurozone that policymakers now deal with both the subdued economy and excessive leverage with force and in a timely manner, avoiding the mistakes of the past.

A credible result of the asset quality review is important, and so is renewed policy action by the ECB. The June 2014 announcement of new measures to repair the broken transmission mechanism and stimulate lending to small and medium enterprises is a welcome signal of its commitment to avoid a persistent undershooting of its inflation target. We advocate that the ECB engage in sizeable quantitative easing as soon as possible. A forceful intervention with outright purchases of sovereign bonds – as well as private securities – is the correct tool for dealing with excessive downward pressure on inflation and fulfils the ECB mandate of price stability while helping the stabilisation of the debt and easing credit conditions. Further procrastination in implementing these by now urgent policy measures would risk, in the medium term, the resurgence of pressures on the sustainability of the Eurozone itself. However, monetary policy is not the appropriate tool to solve debt sustainability and debt overhang problems for which, in extreme cases, some form of debt restructuring should be considered together with adequate structural policies.[28]

Issue 2. Fiscal policy

In this report we have claimed that, in the US, the aggressive fiscal response in the aftermath of the crisis helped households to deleverage without an excessive fall in consumption. Indeed, the literature has pointed to a large fiscal multiplier at the zero lower bound (for recent evidence, see Christiano et al., 2014). The cost of this policy, however, has been rapidly expanding public debt. At the beginning of 2011, government consumption started declining again and the deficit-to-GDP ratio has more than halved since 2009. An important policy question is whether fiscal policy is now too restrictive in the US and is possibly a contributory factor to the weakness of the recovery. The answer to this question depends on the estimate of the size of the multiplier. Although such estimates are highly uncertain, it is likely that with the interest rate departing from the zero lower bound and the end of the deleveraging process, the multiplier is lower

---

28 In relation to the private sector, efficient bankruptcy and insolvency arrangements can facilitate the restructuring of household, corporate and bank debt. In relation to sovereign debt, CIEPR (2013) provides an overview of proposals to improve sovereign debt restructuring mechanisms, while Paris and Wyplosz (2014) outline a potential role for the ECB in reducing the burden of Eurozone sovereign debt.

now than in 2009. This consideration, coupled with the evolution of the debt-to-GDP ratio, calls for an improvement in fiscal policy rather than fiscal expansion. The political class has much work to do in making the tax system more rational, disciplining tax expenditures, differentiating between the current and capital budgets, and making entitlements generationally fairer.

As for the Eurozone, the new fiscal framework provides an anchor for medium-term fiscal stability, while its focus on the underlying structural fiscal position provides some flexibility to enable countercyclical short-run fiscal management. However, this requires European and national fiscal policymakers to strike the right balance between short-run and medium-run fiscal objectives, which is not easy to pull off, especially given the level of uncertainty about the path for potential output.

Fiscal expansion in China during the crisis has taken the form of off-budget spending by local government, financed by an expansion of bank and non-bank credit. This report discussed the rise in local government debt in Chapter 4 and stressed that the country is still leveraging up. The government is clearly facing the challenge of a slowing economy coupled with a huge surge in debt overhang that poses contingent fiscal risks.

Issue 3. Recapitalisation of banks and the sequence of policies

Bank leverage is a key factor in financial crises. When a crisis erupts, the choice is between early action on recapitalisation or procrastination. As highlighted in Chapter 4, the lesson from the Eurozone and the US experiences is that procrastination must be avoided; timeliness and the sequence of policies matter. The delayed policy action in relation to the recapitalisation of banks in the Eurozone was an act of procrastination that kept insolvent institutions alive. Procrastination, while delaying the deleveraging of the banking sector, did not help to avoid a credit crunch. On the contrary, poorly capitalised banks decreased the amount of credit to the real economy, since banks changed the composition of their assets from loans to government bonds. This happened in a context in which fiscal policy was unsupportive while monetary policy became progressively less effective. Once liquidity issues became less relevant, solvency problems in a large part of the European banking sector persisted and became even worse as a consequence of the second recession. The long-term repo loans at a fixed rate (LTRO) implemented by the ECB, although essential to preventing a meltdown of the banking system, were unable to stimulate banks to increase credit to the real economy since they were used by banks mainly to purchase government bonds. The credit restriction was aggravated by a de facto restriction in monetary policy since 2013 when banks started giving back those loans, thereby inducing a renewed shrinking of the ECB balance sheet at a time when the Fed was expanding its assets under the impulse of its QE3 programme.

The US and European experiences with repairing troubled banking systems provides food for thought for Chinese policymakers who must choose between pre-emptive measures to address excess leverage in the financial sector or delaying action at the current juncture. This decision is made more complicated by the underlying decline in the potential growth rate, which has been temporarily obscured by the boost provided by leverage growth in recent years.

A prudent policy strategy would be to allow growth to slow down towards potential (even tolerating a temporary phase of below-trend growth due to deleveraging), and to communicate to the population that this is unavoidable and necessary for the future of the country. Policymakers could then try to achieve a gradual deleveraging in the bank and non-bank sectors, with the low central government debt enabling fiscal measures to recapitalise and restructure banks (including bringing back onto their balance sheets part of the so-called shadow banking) and possibly to bail out large systemically relevant entities. As mentioned in Section 4.3, the cost for growth would be significant, but such pre-emptive measures might avoid a more devastating crisis episode in the medium term.

Issue 4. The international dimension

Finally, this report has primarily focused on the challenges facing domestic policymakers (national fiscal authorities, the major central banks). There are significant international spillover effects from macroeconomic and financial stability policies, both through financial and trade linkages (see, for example, Ghosh and Ostry, 2014). These linkages bind together the advanced and emerging economies, so that it is in the collective interest to improve cooperation in policy-setting. While there are natural conflicts of interest between creditor and debtor nations in relation to the management of legacy debt issues, the potential gains from international policy coordination should not be ignored.

6 Discussions

Morning discussion

Mathias Dewatripont, *National Bank of Belgium*

Mathias Dewatripont agreed with the general message of the report. He argued that we have observed a decrease in nominal GDP growth both on the price side and the real growth side, which is natural after a financial crisis. This has reduced capacity to pay debt and leverage is indeed a problem.

Looking at the distribution of deleveraging, data from Belgium and the EU show that deleveraging has indeed not started. Belgian household financial liabilities are still increasing, but they are completely dwarfed by the financial assets, especially real estate, though the distribution of assets and liabilities is important. Those who hold assets are not the same as those who have the liabilities, a point made forcefully in Thomas Piketty's book. Nevertheless, the story is not complete given tax incentives for wealthy people to borrow rather than invest their own money. Still, the financial positions of individual households are extremely heterogeneous, especially if we look at debt service to income.

At roughly 60% in 1970, the Belgian debt-to-GDP ratio reached 134% in 1993. Then Belgium did deleverage thanks to the convergence rules attached to Eurozone membership. Just before the crisis, the ratio in Belgium stood at 84%; now it is back at 100%. The point here is that the dynamics of debt can be treacherous. The key is the evolution of debt servicing. Its increase since the crisis is attributed to the collapse of nominal GDP, driven more by the fall in inflation than by the fall in real GDP growth. Debt servicing has increased in spite of a large improvement in the budget deficit, and a reduction could take a few years. The real interest rate also matters for debt servicing. Today's interest rates may be very low, which reduces the debt-servicing burden, but real interest rates are above zero. In the 1970s, when Belgium faced a higher debt burden, real interest rates were negative.

Mark Carey, *Federal Reserve Board*

Mark Carey found the report very interesting, but he would have toned down a little the size of the disaster that we are facing. He argued that the thrust of the report is correct but the situation is not as bad as described.

A key theme of the report is that the world has continued to leverage up even as debt repayment capacity has fallen. Repayment capacity in the report is proxied by the GDP growth rate. It is true that debt has continued to increase – a little bit in developed economies and a lot in developing economies – but it is not really obvious that GDP growth rates have fallen. The report emphasises long spans of nominal GDP growth rates. Since the 1970s, the big decline has been driven by lower inflation. We do not know whether real GDP growth rates are going to fall in the future, but we certainly should not extrapolate from the last few years because the crisis was only really over towards the end of 2012.

The conceptual framework is, to a small degree, a credit risk setup and, to large degree, a macroeconomic setup. Looking at the economy from a 100,000 foot perspective, it is reasonable to say that the debt burden that society can bear is a function of GDP growth. If GDP growth goes up then the debt burden goes down, and if the debt goes up then the debt burden goes up as well. One credit risk perspective would be a version of Merton's model of debt: debt capacity is a function of national value, proxied by the rate of GDP growth, and of volatility of GDP growth. There is very little in the report regarding volatility. Yet one feature of the global economy before the crisis was the Great Moderation, during which the volatility of GDP growth had fallen. In such a world, governments can lever up more.

Why are things not quite so bad? True, debt has gone up, but it is not obvious that the capacity to pay has gone down. There is no obvious downtrend in world real GDP growth. One might argue that the decline in inflation over the past 30 years has increased the burden of outstanding debt. However, if you look at debt in the US, only a small proportion of it is fixed-rate, long-term and non-callable. Therefore, in a falling inflation environment much debt has been called or interest rates have been reset, which should have reduced the debt burden as inflation fell. An exception is US government debt because much of it is fixed-rate and non-callable, but at this point in time, most of what is outstanding has low or moderate interest rates.

The report observes that some countries, such as Japan and China, appear to be overleveraged, but they are getting away with it because debt is mostly held domestically. However, you cannot get away with being overleveraged forever and when adjustment comes, there will be an impact on the real economy.

It is important to consider trends for the most leveraged sectors, not just economies as a whole, because the most leveraged sectors harbour much of the credit risk. At least in the US, much of the deleveraging of the last few years was in the most leveraged sectors, a point that is not widely recognised even by most credit risk analysts. The US has a much more stable leverage situation today than it faced before the crisis, because many of the very highly leveraged entities did not survive the crisis.

Olivier Ginguené, *Pictet Asset Management SA, Geneva*

Olivier Ginguené discussed leverage from the point of view of an investor. He liked that the report is fact-based and found it very relevant for investors.

He also agreed with the permanent shock framework and thought that the measurement of time-varying potential output growth matched well his views of the crisis, including the time-varying capacity to repay debt. However, he did not share the report's alarmist view of emerging economies. The situation is worse in the developed economies than in the emerging economies. Some data inconsistencies plague the comparison of leverage between the US, Europe and the emerging economies. Leverage is overestimated for Europe and the emerging markets relative to the US. Causality is also uncertain – is leverage the reason for low growth, or vice versa?

Ginguené added a few points:

- The increase in leverage in emerging economies is largely a Chinese phenomenon.
- Given that nominal interest rates and nominal GDP growth are strongly co-integrated, it is appropriate to use a time-varying discount factor as is done in the report.
- If the trend is set without considering the crisis, then the results are very different from if the trend is calculated including the crisis. When including the crisis, the permanent shock can be interpreted as the adjustment of excess growth and leverage before the crisis.
- This is why the direction of causality between leverage and growth becomes quite opaque.
- The debt Laffer curve introduced in the report is quite original and useful.

Atif Mian, *Princeton University*

Atif Mian agreed that we have not yet seen a significant deleveraging at the global level or a decline in debt. Instead, we have seen a continuous increase in leverage along with a decline in growth, which from a sustainability perspective leaves some questions that need to be addressed.

The fundamental problem we face is two-fold: leverage before and after the crisis. Before the crisis, leverage increased at a time of sustained economic growth, falling real interest rates and no inflationary pressure. After the crisis, as the authors point out, leverage kept rising as private debt turned into public debt and debt levels increased in emerging market economies, such as China. Debt could be the fundamental problem; alternatively, debt could be the symptom of deeper problems in the economy.

As noted by Thomas Piketty, the median income in the US has remained stagnant since the 1970s. If income accumulates at the top of the income distribution, increases in savings by already high-saving top earners mean that the economy will have a hard time equilibrating supply and demand, unless there is way to fill the gap by the issuance of more debt. This is what has happened in the US. Leverage is a symptom of the economy trying to balance itself.

The Chinese economy, instead, relied on someone borrowing and buying its goods. Before the crisis, outsiders leveraged and borrowed to buy Chinese goods, but when outsiders stop leveraging then the domestic economy needs to generate the demand for its goods internally, by generating new credit. In the end, China is no different from the US: debt and the current account offset each other.

Next, we need to think carefully what we mean by a growth shock, which plays a central role in the report's narrative. One shock could be supply-driven, associated with slower technological progress. Another possibility is that the crisis reveals a previous slowing down of global demand. We do not have a firm answer, but demand is more likely to be the culprit. When we look at the run-up of debt in the US, we observe that the income distribution really matters. Surprisingly, perhaps, during the peak of the leverage cycle in the US people with declining incomes were the ones borrowing at a higher rate. Resolving that puzzle is crucial, because the long-run implications differ. In particular, we cannot really make statements about debt capacity until we have an answer. Nor can we decide whether the crisis was caused by a Minsky moment after unsustainable debt accumulation, or whether we have entered a period of secular stagnation that requires winding down debts.

Morning general discussion

Luigi Buttiglione sought to reassure the discussants that the potential growth measures are robust. Accepting that there is a lack of consensus that potential growth is slowing down in the US and that the current low interest rate environment can have positive effects, he indicated that the results of the report do not hinge on these considerations. Vincent Reinhart accepted that the traditional debt-to-GDP ratio is a partial measure of leverage. He agreed that it might be important to consider a time-varying discount rate. As far as Greece is concerned, for instance, changing the discount rate does indeed make a big difference.

The ensuing discussion first focused on the assessment of debt capacity and, more specifically, on estimates of GDP, both potential levels and future trends. **Pierre-Olivier Gourinchas** suggested looking not just at nominal variables but also at the evolution of prices. Also, the report should clarify the rate of variation in the estimation of potential output. **Attilio Zanetti** emphasised that we do not really know what the optimal level of debt-to-GDP is. Much more research is needed at the country level, keeping in mind country-specific characteristics. **Cédric Tille** suggested using demographics and productivity to obtain more transparent estimates, a view strongly supported by **Agnès Benassy-Quéré** and **Amlan Roy**.

Many participants noted the need for a more detailed look at debts. Cédric Tille stressed the issue of contingent liabilities. **Attilio Zanetti** noted that the private and public sectors do not always have the same access to credit. In the case of China, for instance, private enterprises do not receive as much credit as the state-owned companies. If market-oriented sectors are allowed access to credit, this in turn generates more leverage, but in this case it reflects a better allocation of resources. **Jean-Pierre Landau** reminded the conference that not only is it a sovereign problem, but it is also relevant for the corporate sector as well and that the asset side of the balance sheet is important as well as the liability side. He urged the authors to explain why the corporate sector is accumulating so many assets. Pursuing this idea, Richard Portes wanted the report to also examine how debt is going to be liquidated in the future.

Katrin Assenmacher thought that the long-term path for interest rates matters a lot, especially as central banks must eventually raise them. She added that there should be a discussion of the currency denomination of debt. Expanding on this line of thought, **Benoît Coeuré** emphasised the need to consider the role played by cross-borders flows when assessing debt sustainability. For instance, Japan is probably the country with the worst debt-to-GDP ratio but the debt is mostly held locally. In contrast, in the Eurozone, capital movements raise concerns for sustainability. **Stefan Gerlach** developed the view that the debt servicing cost is not independent of the growth potential, which calls for a deeper discussion of interest rates. He added that institutional factors play a crucial role too.

Looking at the banking system in Europe, **Harald Hau** observed that widespread bailouts have redistributed wealth from the taxpayer to the most wealthy 1% of households who own a large share of bank equity. **Mourtaza Asad-Syed** asked whether a tax on credit could reduce future excess leverage, emphasising that it is crucial to determine who has to bear the cost of credit.

Amlan Roy stressed the possibility of a self-fulfilling crisis. In this sense, the international debate should not tone down the fact that debt is a big problem and it keeps growing in some countries. He expressed the view that Belgium has the most unsustainable debt of any country in the European Union and that the potential GDP growth differential between France and Germany was a major concern. **Mathias Dewatripont** responded that Belgium may face a particular political risk but its debt sustainability situation has improved, as shown by many indicators, and the country has never defaulted on its debt.

Yi Huang took up the case of China and other emerging countries. He underlined the roles of capital inflows and of carry trade. He also observed that China is working to improve the efficiency of its financial system through the liberalisation of interest rates and of its capital markets.

Finally, **Carlo Monticelli** advised the authors to dig into the policies needed to obtain the necessary quick deleveraging. It would be interesting to connect the failed reduction in deleveraging to the policy responses to the crisis. The failure to deleverage was a result of the huge monetary and fiscal expansions, which were the right policy actions, but they reduced incentives to adjust rapidly, especially in the financial sector.

Lucrezia Reichlin replied by first observing that the report indeed focuses on both liabilities and assets. An extended balance sheet analysis for the Eurozone and the US stresses the differences between the two regions. She also argued that in Japan, corporate debt is relatively high compared to the US while the degree of corporate leveraging is much lower. This element is crucial since it determines the degree of vulnerability of a country when a banking crisis hits. She agreed that distributional issues and the level of debt servicing are very important.

Luigi Buttiglione agreed with Carlo Monticelli that the policy responses to the recent crisis increased the amount of leverage in the system. He also shared the view that the currency denomination of debt is crucial and pointed to the report's analyses of this issue, particularly in the case of China.

Afternoon discussion

Laurence Boone, *Bank of America Merrill Lynch*

Laurence Boone pointed out how late the process of deleveraging has started, largely spurred by new regulation. In Germany it began in 2012, and similarly in France, where most of the deleveraging in banks is happening through the sale of assets. In Spain and Italy, it started very recently through the sale of loans. New regulation seems to have spurred this deleveraging. Still, it has not yet happened in any significant way.

According to a recent ECB study, differences between Europe and the US are small as far as non-financial corporate sector debt (measured as a percentage of GDP) is concerned. This stands in contrast with the report. It is not appreciated enough how differences in bankruptcy laws in Europe and the US affect household deleveraging. In the US, it is relatively simple for a household to default on a mortgage and to walk away from a home, while in Europe the household's entire wealth is wiped out before it defaults on a mortgage. Similarly, corporate bankruptcy law in Europe makes it harder to recognise loses and this has an impact on deleveraging, innovation and growth.

Finally, the monetary policy stance has been much less expansionary in the Eurozone than in the US. When associated with non-financial corporation deleveraging, the result is a fall in inflation, which then negatively affects the ability to pay back debt. This is an important implication of the currently low inflation environment in the Eurozone.

Kiyohiko Nishimura, *University of Tokyo*

Kiyohiko Nishimura focused on demography. He argued the following:
- The demographic bonus has been the source of excessive optimism in the large developed countries.
- The emergence of bubbles and the subsequent crisis have been driven by the demographic change.
- The continuation of demographic change heralds a period of low growth.

A large working-age population relative to the non-working-age population offers a demographic bonus and the unemployment rate is kept relatively low and stable. Output exceeds what it takes to feed the population, leaving room for discretionary consumption and future investment. The developed economies benefitted from a baby boom, medical advancements lowering infant mortality and prolonging life expectancy, and global post-World War II stability. The slow-moving demographic change under way contributed to excessively optimistic expectations of a prosperous society.

In the Anglo-Saxon countries, as well as in Europe and Japan, crises have roughly coincided with a decreasing non-working-age population ratio. Nishimura presented a wealth of data showing this remarkable coincidence.

The policy implications of these observations are profound. They imply that we do not observe a financial leverage cycle but a fundamentals-driven adjustment. Policy should not pursue the futile objective of reversing course; rather, it should aim at smoothing the unavoidable adjustment. For instance, QE is sometimes presented as a way of smoothing out the situation in the face of considerable uncertainty, but it could just be a painkiller used to postpone adjustment.

Fabio Panetta, *Banca d'Italia*

Fabio Panetta wanted to qualify the report's assessment that takes the US policy as the benchmark for good policy. The country's story is a genuine macroeconomic story, which belies a number of risks in financial stability. After 2008, the US authorities reacted boldly to the crisis and the ensuing recession. Economic growth was supported by expansionary fiscal and monetary policies, and an exchange rate depreciation that partly shifted the burden of adjustment to other countries. The much-admired rapid recapitalisation of banks was largely a consequence of these macroeconomic policies. The expectations that the US authorities would not accept a prolonged recession and that the economy would rapidly get back to growth induced investors to participate in the recapitalisation of banks by the private sector, not by the public sector.

These positive effects may have created substantial risks to financial stability risks. First, leverage did not disappear; it was to a large extent simply shifted from the private sector – from households and banks – to the official sector, i.e. the Treasury and the Fed. If we consolidate the private and the public sector including the Fed, then the adjustment was minor. The exit from the current expansionary monetary policy in the US could affect deleveraging. The level of household debt might be sustainable today, but it might become less sustainable, even unsustainable, once monetary policy is normalised, for example when interest rates increase to a more normal level.

Another problem is that the US financial markets are becoming more and more frothy. The report is silent on the number of sectors that make up the 'shadow banking' system, which has increased in size as the banking system has limited its activities. The shadow banking system is less regulated and possibly poorly capitalised; it poses risks to the whole economy. Similarly, the report is silent on the housing sector, which might also be affected by the exit from expansionary policies. The danger now is complacency about the US. Even the Fed agrees that the financial system in the US is highly fragile.

It is true that a major obstacle in dealing with the crisis in the Eurozon is inadequate governance. The adjustments achieved by weak countries are commendable, but much more remains to be done. At the same time, it would be fair to recognise a number of improvements that have been achieved or that are still being promoted and implemented, such as the new set of fiscal rules and the resolution mechanism.

Profound differences between the Eurozone and the US plague comparisons. The US has faced one financial crisis, while the Eurozone was faced with a sequence of financial crises, each with a different timing and features. Addressing the banking and sovereign debt crises is clearly very difficult. Moreover, intervention is more complex in the financial structure of the Eurozone, which is a bank-based system with large banks, than in the US market-based system, where price signals are continuously available and naturally more conducive to prompt policy intervention.

Different statistical and accounting systems also matter. The accounting standards in the Eurozone tend to produce higher bank leverage than in the US. The consolidation technique is different between the FASB and the IFRS. This contributes to the differences in measured leverage and it complicates benchmarking, as the comparison of the two regions' non-financial corporate sectors shows. These heterogeneities and their implications must be recognised.

Real growth also requires attention. An example is the situation in the Netherlands and Italy. In the Netherlands, leverage is high but the country is growing and there is no financial tension. In Italy, leverage (public and private) is much lower but growth languishes.

While concerns about China are justified, we still need to ask what would have happened to the global financial system had China not supported global demand after 2008? Most likely, the global financial system would be in a much worse shape. The adjustment process in the US would have been much more difficult. Furthermore, it seems that the Chinese authorities have the necessary resources to intervene in order to ensure financial stability. China is still a developing country and it needs to grow and generate 10-12 million jobs per year to avoid social tensions.

Finally, the unresolved problems of US debt, the protracted poor growth in the Eurozone and the expansion in leverage in China are the symptoms of the same illness: a global debt overhang, as observed by Claudio Borio. A global view of leverage and of possible policy measures would recognise the externalities of national policies and call some form of international coordination.

Angel Ubide, *(D.E. Shaw Group and Peterson Institute for International Economics*

Angel Ubide argued that there has been a paradigm shift because someone created the ABX index. When the ABX index was created, investors could short the housing market, ABX assets became informationally sensitive and the repo market dried up. Assets and important elements of the economy essentially changed from being white to being black. This led to shadow banking risk aversion and to declining asset values.

Flight increased risk aversion, the US policy response shifted debt from the private to the public sector, lowered interest rates and promoted risk-taking by quantitative easing and forward guidance. There is nothing in this explanation about potential GDP growth, only a shock to asset prices that needs to be reversed. From this point of view, policy has been very successful in the US.

The lack of deleveraging was the whole point of the policy response. The policy transmission mechanism may have increased risk-taking, but then the question is how much risk-taking is too much. We cannot think about leverage without talking about volatility and the insurance that policymakers are selling to the market.

The Fed is telling the markets that interest rates are going to stay low for a long time, and that they will increase very slowly afterwards and then remain at a low level. Market forecasts reveal that the Fed has been convincing. This means that interest rates will indeed remain low, that volatility too will remain low, and that assets prices will be high. Furthermore, given the impact of Thomas Piketty's book, it will be very hard for the Fed to raise interest rates when wage growth is very weak.

In the Eurozone, it took forever to deal with the banks. The ECB failed in its monetary policy, which is why we have the problem of very low inflation today. What happened in the Eurozone was a different monetary policy faced by various countries. The ECB's LTRO programme prevented a collapse but did not add the credit the economy needed.

Regarding China, the report sounds a bit apocalyptic. The Chinese economy is transitioning from one growth model to another. Leverage is very high but it is well funded, the shadow banking sector is small compared to the developed world, there is very little securitisation, a strong external balance and the expansion in debt is quasi-fiscal. If China liberalises the credit markets and the deposit rate, allocation of credit to private firms will improve. Since these firms are much more productive than the state-owned firms, total factor productivity will increase. Ubide thinks the report should be a bit more balanced in the way it discusses China.

More generally, the emerging market economies have been able to borrow a lot of money because the ABS market is not functioning well at the moment. Emerging market economies are filling a $1-2 trillion gap in the bond market that was left by the collapse of the ABS market.

Regarding liquidity, we have learned that central banks need to lend against any kind of collateral, and the ECB was much better equipped to do that than other central banks. It is good to have excess reserves and there is no need to go back to the pre-crisis level of no excess reserves. The crisis has shown that self-insurance works. It is no surprise that many more countries are running current account surpluses and accumulating foreign reserves, including in the Eurozone. The world does not need a sovereign debt restructuring mechanism.

Policy sequencing is key: austerity should come when growth is back, not before. The Eurozone needs to have Eurobonds because its central bank should be willing to implement quantitative easing without waiting two years to reach that conclusion. Finally, the Eurozone should carry out a region-wide fiscal expansion to arrest the fall in potential growth and therefore reduce the debt-to-GDP ratio.

Afternoon general discussion

Part of the discussion concerned sequencing. **Alexander Swoboda** described a caricature of the usual sequencing discussion as prevention, mitigation and resolution. The experience is that we have not prevented the crisis very well, that we mitigated it somewhat and that we have not resolved the problem yet. Claudio Borio has observed that it is never a good time to solve problems or to reform. When you are on the upswing of the credit or leveraging cycle, you don't want to take the 'punch bowl'' away because you might be accused of having aborted the recovery. And when you are in the down phase of the business cycle, it is really not the time for austerity, to put an additional burden on the banks, and so on. Then we find ourselves in a situation where we are damned if we do and damned if we don't. Interest rates have been low and that was necessary for one goal, but we don't dare raise them to prevent the next bubble or crisis and perhaps the next crisis will come. A useful reminder is provided in the summary of the paper '' Resolving Debt Overhang: Political Constraints in the Aftermath of Financial Crises" by Mian et al. (2014), which ends: 'This paper advances the idea that countries become more politically polarised and fractionalised following financial crises reducing the likelihood of major financial reforms precisely when they might have especially large benefits."

Laurence Boone argued that the Eurozone cannot have the same sequencing as the US because it is not a federation. Indeed, in 2010-11 the markets and policymakers were talking about a Eurozone breakup. The UK regulator was asking banks every month about their contingency plans if a breakup were to happen. The Eurozone could have had the same sequencing as the US if it had decided to move to a fiscal union and the debt of the region was serviced by the entire Eurozone GDP. Instead, the debt of Italy is being serviced by the GDP of Italy, and so on. However, once the Eurozone decided to stick with the 'limited liability partnership' that we have today, the sequencing of policies could not proceed in a similar manner to that of the US.

According to **José Luis Malo de Molina**, there is nothing to object to regarding the sequencing proposed in the report, but in practice very important problems arise. The first problem is how to implement a strategy of fiscal consolidation and austerity until the end of the process. Policymakers need from the beginning to have a credible strategy of medium-term fiscal consolidation. We have seen what has happened in Greece, Portugal, Spain and Ireland, where problems of credibility were at the core of the problem from the beginning. Second, in order to sort out the banking system, policymakers need a lot of public money. To do it in a credible way, government balance sheets need to be healthy. If not, it is very hard to implement the sequencing suggested by the report, as it means leaving austerity until the end of the process. Finally, when comparing the size and the timing of the ECB and Fed interventions, the most important factor is the channel. The channels used by the Fed and ECB are different because the markets in the US are different from those in Europe. The kinds of assets that can be purchased by the ECB are different from the ones that can be purchased by the Fed. The guidance channel, an attempt to affect the final prices, is also different. Laurence Boone reinforced this analysis, asking how the ECB can buy assets when there is no commitment from 18 different national treasuries guaranteeing the risk. In the US and the UK, the treasury guarantees the central bank's risks. No treasury has promised such a guarantee in the Eurozone and the only offer was the guarantee of the balance sheet of the EIB, which is relatively small. This is more a political issue than an institutional one.

Edmond Alphandéry picked up on the issue of the monetary policy stance before and after the crisis. He asserted that it is difficult to describe what happened in the US, the EU and in emerging markets without trying to explain the links that exist between the evolution in leveraging and quantitative easing in the US, Japan and the UK and the monetary policy of the ECB. A good guess involves the evolution of capital flows and carry trade. The international monetary system creates a lot of linkages, which has resulted in disequilibria between the regions of the world. The monetary policy of very low interest rates in the US in the 2000s created excessive demand, not just in the US but worldwide. After the crisis, Europe and the rest of the world were forced to react in the same way.

For **Richard Portes**, while the eventual exit from the current very low interest rate policy is warranted, the same is not necessary true about shrinking central bank balance sheets. The choice is presented as being between a balance sheet reduction and an increase in the price. This is not obvious; at least there is a theoretical disagreement about this. Another issue concerns indebtedness. According to Reinhart et al. (2012), historically the debt-to-GDP ratio has been reduced by an increase in the growth rate. However, there is a lot of disagreement about this result; detailed studies say the opposite for the post-World War II period. In addition, the story of secular stagnation implies that interest rates are going to stay low for a long period of time and the problem of debt is so big anymore. **Jacques Delpla** noted that the story up to now has been about the supply of debt. When we talk about too much leverage, we mean that there is too much debt but also too little equity. At least in Europe, regulation is such that everybody wants to buy debt. For example, banks must hold government debt for their reserves, insurance companies must have extremely secure debt, with MiFID regulation a retail investor must invest in safe assets, and Asian central banks buy safe government bonds. Taxation too treats debt more favourably than equity. Shouldn't we be also talking about that?

Many conference participants challenged the view that China is in a highly dangerous situation. **Carlo Monticelli** recalled that China has $4 trillion in foreign reserves. This is an important buffer to cope with both financial shocks and ageing, and a good reason to be less pessimistic about China. Yet another reason to be less pessimistic is the army of peasants that can be turned into factory workers or capital-intensive farmers, with huge potential increases in productivity and effective demand. They are a source of strength for China. This fact can allow the authors to tone down their pessimism on China. The difficulties of the transformation of peasants into workers, and the number of changes of institutions that need to take place in China every year, are mind boggling, but they are mainly politics. **Amlan Roy** disagreed with Carlo Monticelli. He recalled the hukou system that goes back 56 years. The risk now is a shortage of labour after 2021. In fact, China is already exporting inflation to the rest of the world already. Wage inflation in Shenzhen and other cities has been running at 20% per year since 2009, which reduces the profits of companies such as Foxconn, Nike and others. Worldwide food prices, such as soya beans and pork meat, are rising, which hurts countries like Argentina. The hukou system can be solved but the cost to China's government will be roughly $1.3 trillion. Who is going to pay for it – the central or local governments? Until that problem is solved, China's growth rate will be 6-7%. It is not easy to move 400 million workers from agriculture into more productive industries.

Yi Huang observed that the big jump in the Chinese debt-to-GDP ratio since 2008 came mainly from the $4 trillion stimulus package. It took the form of a credit expansion directed at stable and local government investment vehicles. This huge amount of liquidity, which encouraged the buying of land, ended up in domestic banks deposits and, through Hong Kong, in US dollars. Investors then borrowed these US dollars and, in doing so, they bet on a depreciation and on profits from financial intermediation, which is dangerous. This round-trip process is related to financial repression in China and to the way credit is allocated in the domestic economy. This lack of financial development, rather than too much debt, is the reason why the Chinese authorities are now proceeding to financial market liberalisation. To deal with the hukou problem, China is abolishing its one child policy as a way of increasing labour supply and is reforming its system of land property rights.

The authors then reacted to these comments. **Lucrezia Reichlin** first responded to Angel Ubide about the shock to asset prices. The point is that this is not just about potential income but also about asset price volatility. This is important when comparing the US and Eurozone policies. In the US, the sustained quantitative easing policy, combined with easier fiscal policy, made the deleveraging process less painful. Reichlin also accepted the point by José Luis Malo de Molina that sequencing is good in principle but very difficult in practice, especially as there is still no fiscal policy tool in the Eurozone. Even if a Eurozone fiscal policy tool did exist, the question of what would be a credible fiscal framework remains open.

Regarding the issue of dealing with the banks at a very early stage, she disagreed with Fabio Panetta. The first phase of the crisis in the Eurozone was mainly an interbank market story – the interbank market dried out because of counterparty risk. Dealing with banks at an early stage has the advantage of dealing with counterparty risk, establishes clarity and distinguishes between the good and the bad part of the banking system. For a long time, the ECB was providing liquidity to everybody without knowing what was on the balance sheet of each bank. It is only now that we are dealing with that.

The banking system has become very fragmented geographically because we have not been able to deal with sovereign risk and bank risk. No matter what the size of the ECB's balance sheet is, the transmission mechanism does not work because interest rates in Spain, for example, are much higher than in Germany. Even though some progress has now been made with the banking union and other aspects, the Eurozone faces the more traditional issue of low inflation. The tools used by the Fed ought to be recognised.

In response to Laurence Boone's comments regarding non-financial corporations, Lucrezia Reichlin indicated that she is aware of the difference between the report's numbers and those presented by the ECB. The report looks at non-consolidated debt in both the US and the Eurozone, while the ECB might not be using the non-consolidated debt measure. The difficulties in comparing the data mean that the focus should be on adjustment. On this measure, differences remain. In the US, non-financial corporations have behaved in a very cyclical manner. In the Eurozone, non-financial corporations have adjusted to a certain extent, through an accumulation of liquidity and excess savings similar to that which happened previously in Japan.

Of course, the Eurozone could not have done what the US has done. The question is the price that has been paid for this, and the answer should inform institutional reform and the need for tools to allow the ECB to navigate the protracted low inflation environment. On the other hand, it is not certain that Treasury guarantees on government bond risk are an issue.

Regarding demographics, Reichlin mentioned the potential importance of immigration. Demographics have been a big problem for Japan, and might also be a problem for the Eurozone.

Luigi Buttiglione reiterated that policy sequencing has proven to be very difficult in the Eurozone. The UK fared better by tackling the medium-term needs of the public sector balance sheet without killing the economy in the short term. This was possible thanks to better institutions and politics, but also through currency depreciation. Regarding Edmond Alphandéry's comments about US policy and its global effects, he agreed that the excessive expansion of leverage was, ex post, the wrong policy in the US between 2004 and 2008. In response to Richard Portes, Buttiglione pointed out that the ratio of debt to GDP has either gone up or at best stabilised during periods of very low interest rates. The low interest rate environment has not been used to achieve deleveraging and this is a source of fragility.

Regarding China, he noted that immigration from the countryside to the cities is slowing down quite a lot. This is perhaps by design and it is unclear what will happen in the future. Published data show a combination of an accelerating debt-to-GDP ratio and decelerating nominal GDP. This is a pretty poisonous combination.

Large Chinese foreign reserves are considered a source of strength, but one needs to qualify this. The rotation from investment to consumption, from the demand to the supply side, or from manufacturing to services or wages to profits, may lead to more stable growth but also to less growth. This may well be the right thing to do, but what about the existing high level of debt, which was contracted when expectations about future investment and output growth rates were higher? It is not encouraging to see where the new debt has gone. This is the reason why the new debt has not been translated into an acceleration of the growth rate. To the contrary, the acceleration of the debt growth rate has gone hand-in-hand with a deceleration in the output growth rate.

Summarising, **Benoît Coeuré** observed a consensus that leverage cycles matter enormously. It was also agreed that understanding past leverage cycles is important to prepare for the future in terms of policies and institutions, which is vital for the Eurozone. He noted wide agreement that the policy sequencing was right in the US but not in Europe. Disagreements arise over whether the European failure should be attributed to institutions, to policy mistakes, or to both. He further observed that the role of demography may be more important than is usually recognised. He opined that redistributive issues and inequality also matter a lot. He expressed hope that disagreements about the measure of debt would be resolved. Finally, he noted that controversy was part of the process.

Data Appendix

Debt typically expressed as a ratio to GDP, where GDP data are from the IMF.

Debt variables

General government
Source for Austria, Belgium, Cyprus, Finland, France, Germany, Greece, Ireland, Italy, Luxembourg, Netherlands, Portugal and Spain: Eurostat. Source for other countries: IMF World Economic Outlook 2014.

Households
"Loans" category in non-consolidated stocks of liabilities for sector "Households and non-profit institutions serving households". Source: OECD Financial Balance Sheets database.

Note: 2013 values are estimated based on the available quarterly data for Austria, Czech Republic, Denmark, Finland, France, Germany, Ireland, Italy, Japan, Korea, Netherlands and Spain. Data for Switzerland are for 2012.

Non-financial corporates
Sum of "Loans" and "Securities other than shares, except financial derivatives" categories in non-consolidated stock of liabilities for sector "Non-financial corporations". Source: OECD Financial Balance Sheets database.

Note: 2013 values are estimated based on the available quarterly data for Austria, Czech Republic, Denmark, Finland, France, Germany, Ireland, Italy, Japan, Korea, Netherlands and Spain. Data for Switzerland are for 2012.

Financial corporates
Sum of "Loans" and "Securities other than shares, except financial derivatives" categories in non-consolidated stock of liabilities for sector "Financial corporations". Source: OECD Financial Balance Sheets database.

Note: 2013 values are estimated based on the available quarterly data for Austria, Czech Republic, Denmark, Finland, France, Germany, Ireland, Italy, Japan, Korea, Netherlands and Spain. Data for Switzerland are for 2012.

Total
Sum of debt levels for government, household and non-financial corporates.

Total ex-financial
Sum of debt levels for government, household and non-financial corporates.

Total private ex-financial
For developed economies: sum of debt levels for households and non-financial corporates.

For emerging markets: Sum of credit to private sector (National sources & IMF) and debt securities issued by non-financial corporations (source: BIS international debt securities database).

For China: total social financing (CEIC databank)

Other variables

Net external position
Source: IMF.

External Debt
Source: BIS external debt statistics.

Net international investment position
Source: IMF.

Total social financing - China
Source: CEIC databank.

Country groups

Developed markets (DM) are Australia, Austria, Belgium, Canada, Denmark, Finland, France, Germany, Greece, Ireland, Italy, Japan, Netherlands, New Zealand, Norway, Portugal, Spain, Sweden, Switzerland, UK and US (21 countries).

Emerging markets (EM) are Argentina, Brazil, Bulgaria, Chile, China, Colombia, Czech Republic, Hungary, India, Indonesia, Israel, Korea, Malaysia, Mexico, Philippines, Poland, Russia, South Africa, Thailand, Turkey and Ukraine (21 countries comprising EM1 and EM2).

Emerging markets 1 (EM1) are Argentina, Brazil, Chile, India, Indonesia, Russia, South Africa and Turkey (8 countries).

Emerging markets 2 (EM2) are Bulgaria, China, Colombia, Czech Republic, Hungary, Israel, Korea, Malaysia, Mexico, Philippines, Poland, Thailand and Ukraine (13 countries).

References

Adrian, T., E. Moench and H. S. Shin (2013), "Leverage Asset Pricing", Federal Reserve Bank of New York Staff Report No. 625.

Arellano, C. and N. Kocherlakota (2014), "Internal Debt Crises and Sovereign Default", *Journal of Monetary Economics*, forthcoming.

Banbura, M., D. Giannone and L. Reichlin (2010), "Large Bayesian VARs", *Journal of Applied Econometrics* 25(1), pp. 71-92.

Battistini, N., M. Pagano and S. Simonelli (2014), "Systemic Risk, Sovereign Yields and Bank Exposures in the Euro Crisis", *Economic Policy* 29, pp. 203-251.

Bernanke, B. and M. Gertler (1989), "Agency Costs, Net Worth and Business Fluctuations", *American Economic Review* 79(1), pp. 14-31.

Blanchard, O. and F. Giavazzi (2002), "Current Account Deficits in the Euro Area: The End of the Feldstein Horioka Puzzle?", *Brookings Papers on Economic Activity* 33(2), pp. 147-210.

Borio, C., R. N. McCauley and P. McGuire (2011), "Global Credit and Domestic Credit Booms", *BIS Quarterly Review*, September, pp. 43–57.

Brown, M. and P. R. Lane (2011), "Debt Overhang in Emerging Europe?", World Bank Policy Research Working Paper No. 5784.

Brunnermeier, M. and Y. Sannikov (2014), "A Macroeconomic Model with a Financial Sector", *American Economic Review* 104(2), pp. 379-421.

Bruno, V. and H.S. Shin (2014), "Globalization of Corporate Risk Taking", *Journal of International Business Studies*, forthcoming.

Catão, L. and G.M. Milesi-Ferretti (2013), "External Liabilities and Crises", IMF Working Paper No. 13/113.

Cerra, V. and S. C. Saxena (2008), "Growth Dynamics: The Myth of Economic Recovery", *American Economic Review* 98(1), pp. 439–457.

Checherita, C. and P. Rother (2010), "The impact of high and growing government debt on economic growth: An empirical investigation for the euro area", ECB Working Paper No. 1237.

Christiano, L. J., M. S. Eichenbaum and M. Trabandt (2014), "Understanding the Great Recession", NBER Working Paper No. 20040.

Cochrane, J. H. (2011), "Discount Rates", *Journal of Finance* 66(4), pp. 1047-1108.

Committee on International Economic Policy and Reform (CIEPR) (2013), *Revisiting Sovereign Bankruptcy*, Washington, DC: Brookings Institution.

Cordella, T., L. A. Ricci and M. Ruiz-Arranz (2005), "Debt overhang or debt irrelevance? revisiting the debt-growth link", IMF Working Paper No. 05/223.

Corsetti, G., K. Kuester, A. Meier and G. Muller (2013), "Sovereign Risk, Fiscal Policy and Macroeconomic Stability", *Economic Journal* 123(566), pp. 99-132.

Dash, M. (1999), *Tulipomania: The Story of the World's Most Coveted Flower and the Extraordinary Passions it Aroused*, New York: Crown Publishers.

David, P. (1989), "The Dynamo and the Computer: An Historical Perspective on the Modern Productivity Paradox", *American Economic Review* 80(2), pp. 355-361.

De Mol, C., D. Giannone and L. Reichlin (2008), "Forecasting using a large number of predictors: Is Bayesian shrinkage a valid alternative to principal components?", *Journal of Econometrics* 146(2), pp. 318-328.

Devereux, M. B., P. R. Lane and J. Xu (2006), "Exchange Rates and Monetary Policy for Emerging Market Economies", *Economic Journal* 116(511), pp. 478-506.

Eggertsson, G. and P. Krugman (2012), "Debt, Deleveraging, and the Liquidity Trap: A Fisher-Minsky-Koo Approach", *Quarterly Journal of Economics* 127(3), pp. 1469-1513.

European Central Bank (2012), "Corporate Indebtedness in the Euro Area", *Monthly Bulletin*, February, pp. 87-103.

Farhi, E., P.O. Gourinchas and H. Rey (2011), *Reforming the International Monetary System*, London: Centre for Economic Policy Research.

Fisher, I. (1933), "The Debt-Deflation Theory of Great Depressions", *Econometrica* 1, p. 337.

Fostel, A. and J. Geanakoplos (2013), "Leverage, Securitization and Shadow Banking: Theory and Policy", mimeo, George Washington University.

Furceri, D. and A. Mourougane (2009), "The Effect of Financial Crises on Potential Output: New Empirical Evidence", OECD Economics Department Working Paper No. 699.

Furceri, D. and A. Zdzienicka (2012), "Banking Crises and Short and Medium Term Output Losses in Emerging and Developing Countries: The Role of Structural and Policy Variables", *World Development* 40(12), pp. 2369-2378.

Ghosh, A. and J. Ostry (2014), "Obstacles to International Policy Coordination, And How to Overcome Them", mimeo, International Monetary Fund.

Giannone, D., M. Lenza and L. Reichlin (2011), "Market Freedom and the Global Recession", *IMF Economic Review* 59(1), pp. 111-135.

Giannone, D., M. Lenza and G. Primiceri (2010), "Prior Selection for Vector Autoregressions", CEPR Discussion Paper No. 8755.

Giannone, D., M. Lenza and L. Reichlin (2012), "The ECB and the Interbank Market", *Economic Journal* 122(564), pp. 467-486.

Gourinchas, P.O. and M. Obstfeld (2012), "Stories of the Twentieth Century for the Twenty-First", *American Economic Journal: Macroeconomics* 4(1), pp. 226-65.

Imbs, J. and R. Ranciere (2008) "The Overhang Hangover", mimeo, Paris School of Economics.

International Monetary Fund (2014a), *Global Financial Stability Report* (April).

International Monetary Fund (2014b), *World Economic Outlook* (April).

Jorda, O., M. Schularick and A. M. Taylor (2011)," Financial Crises, Credit Booms, and External Imbalances: 140 Years of Lessons", *IMF Economic Review* 59(2), pp. 340-378.

Jorda, O., M. Schularick and A. M. Taylor (2013), "When Credit Bites Back", *Journal of Money, Credit and Banking* 45(s2), pp. 3-28.

Kindleberger, C. P. and R. Z. Aliber (2011), *Manias, Panics and Crashes: A History of Financial Crises*, 6th edition, London: Palgrave Macmillan.

Krugman, P. (1988), "Financing versus Forgiving Debt Overhang", *Journal of Development Economics* 29, pp. 253-268.

Krugman, P. (2014), "Inflation Targets Reconsidered," mimeo, Princeton University.

Kumar, M. S. and J. Woo (2010) "Public Debt and Growth", IMF Working Paper 10/174.

Laeven, L. and T. Laryea (2009), "Principles of Household Debt Restructuring", IMF Staff Position Note 09/15.

Lane, P. R. (2013), "Capital Flows in the Euro Area", European Economy Economic Paper No. 497.

Lane, P. R. and G. M. Milesi-Ferretti (2007), "The External Wealth of Nations Mark II", *Journal of International Economics* 73(2), pp. 223-250.

Lane, P. R. and G. M. Milesi-Ferretti (2011), "The Cross-Country Incidence of the Global Crisis", *IMF Economic Review* 59(1), pp. 77-110.

Lane, P. R. and G. M. Milesi-Ferretti (2012), "External Adjustment and the Global Crisis", *Journal of International Economics* 88(2), pp. 252-265.

Lane, P. and G. M. Milesi-Ferretti (2014), "Global Imbalances and External Adjustment after the Crisis", IMF Working Paper No. 14/151.

Lane, P. R. and P. McQuade (2014), "Domestic Credit Growth and International Capital Flows", *Scandinavian Journal of Economics* 116(1), pp. 218-252.

Lane, P. R. and B. Pels (2012), "Current Account Imbalances in Europe", *Moneda y Credito* 234, pp. 225-261.

Lane, P. R. and J. Shambaugh (2010), "The Long or Short of It: Determinants of Foreign Currency Exposure in External Balance Sheets", *Journal of International Economics* 80(1), pp. 33-44.

Laryea, T. (2010), "Approaches to corporate debt restructuring in the wake of financial crises", IMF Staff Discussion Note 10/02.

Martin, P. and T. Philippon (2014), "Inspecting the Mechanism: Leverage and the Great Recession in the Eurozone", mimeo, Sciences Po.

McKinsey Global Institute (2010), *Debt and Deleveraging: The Global Credit Bubble and Its Economic Consequences.*

Melzer, B. (2010), "Mortgage Debt Overhang: Reduced Investment by Homeowners with Negative Equity", mimeo, Kellogg School of Management.

Mendoza, E. (2010), "Sudden Stops, Financial Crises and Leverage", *American Economic Review* 100(5), pp. 1941-1966.

Mian, A. and A. Sufi (2014), *House of Debt: How They (and You) Caused the Great Recession, and How We Can Prevent it from Happening Again*, Chicago, IL: University of Chicago Press.

Midrigan, Y. and T. Philippon (2012), "Household Leverage and the Recession", mimeo, New York University.

Mulligan, C. B. (2008) "A Depressing Scenario: Mortgage Debt Becomes Unemployment Insurance", NBER Working Paper No. 14514.

Myers, S. (1977), "The Determinants of Corporate Borrowing", *Journal of Financial Economics* 5(2), pp. 147-175.

Olney, M. L. (1999), "Avoiding Default: The Role of Credit in the Consumption Collapse of 1930", *Quarterly Journal of Economics* 114(1), pp. 319-335.

Paris, P. and Wyplosz, C. (2014), *PADRE: Politically Acceptable Debt Restructuring in the Eurozone*, Geneva Reports on the World Economy, Special Report 3, London: CEPR and Geneva: ICMB.

Rajan, R. (2010), *Fault Lines: How Hidden Fractures Still Threaten the World Economy*, Princeton, NJ: Princeton University Press.

Reichlin, L. (2014), "Monetary Policy and Banks in the Euro Area: The Tale of Two Crises", *Journal of Macroeconomics* 39(PB), pp. 387-400.

Reinhart, C. M. and K. S Rogoff (2009), "The Aftermath of Financial Crises", *American Economic Review* 99(2), pp. 466-72.

Reinhart, C. M. and K. S. Rogoff (2010), "Growth in a Time of Debt", *American Economic Review* 100(2), pp. 573–578.

Reinhart, C. M. and V. R. Reinhart (2010), "The Decade After the Fall: Diminished Expectations, Double Dips, and External Shocks", VoxEU.org, 13 September.

Reinhart, C. M. and M. B. Sbrancia (2014), "The Liquidation of Government Debt," *Economic Policy*, forthcoming.

Reinhart, C. M., V. R. Reinhart and K. S. Rogoff (2012), "Public Debt Overhangs: Advanced-Economy Episodes since 1800", *Journal of Economic Perspectives* 26(3), pp. 69-86.

Sachs, J. D. (1989), "Conditionality, Debt Relief, and the Developing Country Debt Crisis", in J. D. Sachs (ed.), *Developing Country Debt and the World Economy*, Chicago, IL: University of Chicago Press.

Shin, H. S. (2013), "The Second Phase of Global Liquidity and Its Impact on Emerging Markets", mimeo, Princeton University.

Stein J. C. (2012), "Evaluating Large-Scale Asset Purchases", speech at the Brookings Institution, Washington, DC, 11 October.

Summers, L. (2013), "Secular Stagnation," speech at the 14th IMF Annual Research Conference, Washington, DC, 8 November.

Tirole, J. (2012), "Country Solidarity, Private Sector Involvement and the Contagion of Sovereign Crises", mimeo, Toulouse University.